IT ARCHITECT SERIES™

Stories from the Field

Horror stories and lessons learned from IT Architects, Operations, and Project Management.

Editors

Matthew Wood, Editor-in-Chief
John Yani Arrasjid, Editor
Mark Gabryjelski, Editor

Upper Saddle River, NJ • Boston • Indianapolis • San Francisco • New York • Toronto • Montreal • London • Munich • Paris • Madrid • Cape Town • Sydney • Tokyo • Singapore • Mexico City

IT Architect Series: Stories from the Field

Published by IT Architect Resource, LLC
14 Ansel Street, Salem, New Hampshire 03079
itaseries.com

The opinions expressed in this book belong to the writers (contributors, editors, and artist) and are not necessarily those of the companies they work for.

Warning and Disclaimer

Every effort has been made to make this book as complete and as accurate as possible, but no warranty or fitness is implied. The information provided is on an “as is” basis. The authors and the publisher shall have neither liability nor responsibility to any person or entity with respect to any loss or damages arising from the information contained in this book.

ISBN: 978-0-9990929-1-0 (ePub)
ISBN: 978-0-9990929-2-7 (sc)

Library of Congress Control Number: 2020914263

Rev. Date: 7/28/2020

Dedication

In 2020, we started off with a huge challenge, a pandemic. Although a pandemic does not immediately affect technologies, it does affect people and the processes that people use with technology. It has affected everyone. In the tech industry, where we have been using remote work tools such as online conferencing, it is possible to work at home. Not everyone is as fortunate, including all the front-line workers that are helping the world get through the crisis. We will see new lessons learned from both successes and failures in this process. I would like to dedicate this book to all those who are working to help others including essential workers in emergency services, medical services, food distribution, and pharmacies. Our best wishes are for the world to be successful in both health and work, and for being compassionate to those in need.

“You don’t always notice,
the miles roll by as you run,
but there’s a time for looking back,
to see how far you’ve come.”

Contents

Acknowledgements

Building a book that is a collection of stories is not without challenges. Different languages, cultures, perspectives, and roles have all played an important part in the diversity of the contributors and the stories. The editors would like to thank the following people for their support in developing and reviewing the material in this collection.

Special thanks to family and friends who supported our efforts in creating this work. Thank you to Ioannis Dangerous Age for the incredible artwork for the cover of the book, and to Matthew Wood for his editorial work and help evolving the stories.

I worked with Matthew on previous books such as the *vCloud Architecture Toolkit* (vCAT). We worked together to complete the final phase of the stories, including some ghost writing to enhance the material.

My friend Ioannis Dangerous Age is an artist well known in the music industry. He has worked with several of my favorite musicians, and I enjoy his work on the pieces I own. We first met through a Kickstarter project called "Get the Led Out" by Denny Somach. We also worked on a Jean-Michel Cousteau project that resulted in a 3D IMAX movie in 2019. Through this friendship I have gotten to meet personally with Jean-Michel Cousteau, Jean-Michel Jarre, and Jon Anderson. His biography includes more details, including how to order cover art prints.

The full list of contributors and reviewers is provided in the Stories Preface. Thank you to each and every one of you for your dedication on writing, reviewing, and revising the stories, and thanks to reviewers for providing valuable feedback.

Thank you to our families and friends for support on this and many other fun projects. Love you!

John Yani Arrasjid, VCDX-001

Foreword

One of the ways that many of us continue to learn and grow to stay relevant and sharp is from participation in the "community." I have been involved with the virtualization and larger technology community for over ten years and I am as passionate about it now as I ever was. With so many people in the community, I am not unique in this way. I think we participate and contribute to the community because we learn from each other and grow our skills together. This is why I got involved in the VMware User Group (VMUG) and stayed invested all these years.

No-one does anything for a decade or longer without a reason. Ten years is a long time – even for those of us fortunate enough to live a full century, it is a significant portion of a lifetime. For anyone to commit to something that long there must be a reason for it. For example, anyone who has spent ten years studying martial arts is unlikely to wake up one morning and question why they are heading to the dojo. It is because they are passionate about the sport and want to be part of that community. It is intentional.

Many of us who have eclipsed the ten-year mark in our IT careers can tell you that it is not an accident: we are committed to advancing our organizations through technology and process improvement. Unlike a lot of careers, rapid change is endemic to IT and requires consistent learning and growth to stay relevant. Many of you may be focused on your third, fourth, or even tenth different technical focus since starting your career. And to keep that edge you must acquire new knowledge and skills while simultaneously applying the ones you already have to projects and operations that move our organizations forward. Staying relevant in IT requires intentional effort and disciplined learning; otherwise, you end up telling people you "used to work in IT."

The community gives those involved access to training, mentoring, career opportunities, skill building, and friendship. I look forward to industry events like VMworld or VMUG UserCons, not just because I get to talk shop with people and learn about and play with new software or solutions, but also because I get to connect with people who are invested in each other. We care about each other. That is the magic of being a part of the community. It does not just give us a chance to grow; it also gives us an opportunity to train, mentor, develop, and invest in others.

The most powerful aspect of being a part of the cloud/virtualization/technology community is that we share experiences with each other. I sometimes think of a career in technology to be like a hike in the mountains. There are lots of paths that often cross, and you have to pick one you think you will enjoy the best. In my experience, having an experienced guide helps. Being in the tech community means that you do not have to go down the metaphorical path alone or blaze a new trail without a guide map. Some of us have been that way before, and we can tell you where to step and where *not* to step. The community can tell you where disaster lurks and where we have had successes. Ultimately, being in the community means that you do not have to go it alone, that you have people by your side that care about you and your success. Not because you work for the same logo or are invested in the same project, but because they care about you as an individual.

The community is not just about conferences, events, and Twitter (though these are big pieces of it.) The community can take many shapes and has many different aspects to it. Some people contribute by speaking, some by blogging, and others play a role by organizing webinars or producing podcasts. And some organize a team of people to write a book...

What you are holding in your hands is a product of the community. This fourth book of the IT Architect series is all about people who have been down the path reporting back on their experiences and the lessons they have learned, lessons that they want to share with you. Thirty-five professionals representing hundreds of years of experience have taken the time to give you the benefit of their experience so that you do not need to learn the hard way. In many cases, they tell you what they would not do again.

Ultimately, this book is a collection of wisdom gained the hard way, and any time that you are presented with wisdom, take the opportunity to learn. Read it with a highlighter, take notes in the margins, digest every detail, and think through what you would do differently. Every contributor has given you something that they learned, but perhaps you learned something additional from their story; do not discount that, make that knowledge a part of what you bring to your role. Most importantly, I urge you to listen to these stories not just as cautionary tales, but as opportunities to skip the bad part of experiential learning. You can accelerate your career without incurring the pain that we went through.

So, grab a cup of coffee and get ready to get a crash course in project management, architecture, design, operations, and more as you hear from those reporting back from the field on what is down that metaphorical path.

Steve Athanas, VMUG President
@steveathanas
www.transformationaltechnologist.com

Stories Preface

Projects present challenges. How you deal with a challenge, even if it involves a major or catastrophic disaster, is critical. It is important to learn what could be done differently to avoid the failure, and to share what you learn with others. This book is a collection of stories contributed by your colleagues to share experiences and lessons learned on challenging IT projects. Failures are described in detail, along with insights and solutions, so that you might learn from their mistakes and avoid similar issues.

I take great pleasure in presenting this collection of stories from contributors around the globe. The stories and projects span topics that include technical, operational, financial, and other areas. See the Topic Codes section for a list of codes used to describe each story.

As we developed the concept of this book, Mark Gabryjelski and I brainstormed on how we could structure an entertaining and informative collection of stories. We included technology, but focused primarily on the contributor's experiences and lessons learned. This book complements other books in the IT Architect Series by sharing knowledge related to IT architecture with the community.

Many of the story headings are standardized with questions that lead to a critical examination of the issues.

- What was the project?
- What was the failure?
- How did it impact my customer?
- What could I have done differently?
- What did I learn?

For this collaborative effort, contributors agreed to write stories without direct attribution. These are stories about real projects, so customer and author names (and some vendor names) were removed to preserve anonymity. We also anonymized other details so that no confidential information is included.

These stories have evolved through the efforts of many reviewers and the editorial team. Most contributors helped with cross-reviews of stories and contributed feedback that significantly improved presentation and technical accuracy.

In my work over the last two decades, I have encountered situations and outcomes similar to those described in the stories. I expect that there is at least one story that will elicit similar memories from a project you have worked on in the past.

We took a different approach for this book. It has technical and operational content, but is *not* a technical book like *Foundation in the Art of Infrastructure Design*. The stories are informative, but are also intended to be entertaining.

If you are interested in contributing to our next book, *Stories from the Field, Volume 2*, please reach out to me directly.

John Yani Arrasjid, 2020

Contributors and Reviewers

For this book we endeavored to create a collection of real-life stories that are entertaining and relevant, and provide lessons learned in planning technical environments. We called out to the industry and our community for stories. We also reached out to individuals at conferences. Many are recognized by their certifications and titles. Leading IT architects from around the world contributed their stories to the collection. Together, the editing team (Matthew Wood, John Arrasjid, and Mark Gabryjelski) and most contributors reviewed and shared creative feedback that was incorporated to round out each story.

Biographies of contributors can be found on the IT Architect Resource, LLC website: itaseries.com

The following people participated on this project.

Abdullah Abdullah - contributor, reviewer
Johan van Amersfoort – contributor
John Yani Arrasjid - Editor and contributor
Steve Athanas – Foreword, contributor
Doug Baer – contributor, reviewer
Marco van Baggum - contributor, reviewer
René van den Bedem – contributor
Daemon Behr – contributor
Hans Bernhardt – contributor
Michael Berthiaume – contributor
Jayson Block – contributor, reviewer
Wayne Conrad – contributor, reviewer
Paul Cradduck – contributor, reviewer
Sachin Dharmadhikari – contributor, reviewer
Tony Foster – contributor
Mark Gabryjelski - Editor and contributor
Faisal Hasan – contributor, reviewer
Ray Heffer – contributor, reviewer
John Kozej – contributor, reviewer
Christopher Kusek – contributor
Sean Massey – contributor, reviewer
Wences Michel – contributor, reviewer
Christian Mohn – contributor, reviewer (Proact IT Norge AS)
Geoffrey O'Brien – contributor, reviewer
Josh Odgers – contributor, reviewer
David Quinney – contributor, reviewer
Bas Raayman – contributor, reviewer
Yves Sandfort – contributor
Rachit Srivastava – contributor, reviewer
Jorge Torres – contributor, reviewer
Raman Veeramraju – contributor
Matthew Wood – Editor-in-Chief and contributor
Szymon Ziolkowski – contributor, reviewer
Chip Zoller – contributor, reviewer
Dorine Arrasjid – reviewer
Steve Bochinski – reviewer
Kirkland Brown – reviewer
Rudi van Drunen – reviewer
Darrel Carson – reviewer
Kenneth Moore – reviewer
Ioannis Dangerous Age – cover design

Topic Codes

Use the following topic codes to identify stories that cover areas of interest to you. The primary topic area (and sometimes a second prominent topic area) is highlighted for each story. For example, **BCDR**.

Code	Description
$	Financial or budgetary.
ANALYSIS	Incorrect analysis in design, implementation, or testing.
AUTO	Automation.
AVAIL	Availability.
BCDR	Business Continuity and Disaster Recovery.
CHANGE	Change Management or transformation.
COMM	Interpersonal communication, soft skills.
DB	Database.
EUC	End-User Computing. Virtual desktop-related.
NETWORK	Network-related.
OPS	Operations- and facilities-related.
PERSP	Differences in perspective of architect, team, and stakeholder.
POLITICS	Related to politics.
RCA	Requirements, Constraints, Assumptions.
ROBO	Remote Office or Back Office.
RISK	Risk management and mitigation.
SALES	Mismatch between what was sold and what was delivered.
SEC	Security, viruses, and social engineering.
SCOPE	Related to scope creep, failed SOWs, and conflicting priorities.
SKILL	Skills mismatch. Lack of training.
STAKEHOLDER	Stakeholder issues.
STORAGE	Storage-related.
SUPPORT	Support issues.
TIME	Time-related, including life/work balance.
TRUST	Trust related to others you depend on.
WAR	War-related considerations impacting design.

A Quick Guide to the Stories

The following is a brief description of each story, classified by topic codes.

$, BCDR, OPS, RISK

Location, Location, Location

Water, water, everywhere.... How do liquids and datacenters mix? What happens when planning, budget, and risk management fail to prevent a disaster.

RCA, RISK, SCOPE, SUPPORT, TIME, TRUST

Prerequisites and Project Plans Matter

What would you do if you arrive at the project site and find that the prerequisites are not complete and there is a change in the technology? And the issues just keep coming.... Do you push back?

ANALYSIS, EUC, RISK, SCOPE, TIME, TRUST

An Architect's VDI aPOCalypse

An architect learns to always write a design doc, even during a VDI POC. What you do not know *can* hurt you!

$, ANALYSIS, COMM, RCA, RISK, SCOPE, TIME

A Murphy's Law Datacenter Migration

A datacenter migration is a significant undertaking and preparation is critical to success. Failure to plan any aspect of a migration can and will result in catastrophe that affects everything. Systematic preparation is fundamental and helps you and your team avoid a negative outcome.

EUC, NETWORK, PERSP, RISK, STORAGE, TIME, TRUST

Creatures of Habit

Just because it has always been done that way does not mean that you should do it the same way the next time. While onsite delivering a design for a large business-critical VDI environment, a last-minute change put the successful completion of the design at risk, and there was no time to test the change. When the project team insisted on going ahead with the change, the architect started to second-guess his own knowledge and experience.

ANALYSIS, COMM, PERSP, RCA, RISK, TRUST

The Oversized Physical Exchange Server Project

This story is about a failed Exchange Server deployment on physical servers, due to incorrect sizing requirements gathered based on incorrect assumptions and an existing virtualized Exchange design. This caused lengthy outages and a large increase in project cost due to the need for additional hardware.

ANALYSIS, COMM, EUC, PERSP, RCA, STAKEHOLDER

Realize What Customers Are Not Telling You

We built a brand-new VDI environment for our university, and realized on launch day that we had missed a key use case. All requirements must be discovered, especially the unspoken ones.

ANALYSIS, DB, RCA, SALES, STORAGE

The Workload and Requirements Matter

Finding yourself unexpectedly on the wrong side of the 80/20 rule can be a painful experience when the requirements have not been properly gathered. Missing a critical piece of the puzzle can result in a spectacular failure, even when everything else is planned and executed flawlessly.

CHANGE, PERSP, POLITICS, RCA, SCOPE

Design for the Right People

Developing a Cloud Management Platform (CMP) with multiple stakeholders, each with different perspectives and motivations, can pose a challenge. Lack of communication has a negative impact on projects. Knowing who to work with, establishing status calls for checkpoints to ensure alignment, and avoiding too many "cooks" is essential for successful outcomes.

EUC, NETWORK, RCA

If You Want to Win You Must Lose

Remember that day you made some bad assumptions, built a flawed solution, and pulled the wrong cables taking down a VDI environment? I hope you have not experienced such a day, but I have and I invite you to learn from my mistakes. This story is a companion story to *You Own It All.*

BCDR, DB, SCOPE

You Own It All

Some architects assume they have all of the answers and do not really listen to their clients. Other architects might fail to ask all of the necessary questions due to a lack of confidence. Is it a lack of humility that causes us to overcompensate? Be humble enough to ask all of the questions, discover all of the requirements, and deliver the best possible outcomes for your clients.

ANALYSIS, AVAIL, BCDR, COMM, OPS, PERSP, RISK

The Underground Fire

Under the city there is a story to be told by contemporary archaeologists. It is a history of unseen tunnels with wires and cables that make our modern civilization possible. In this story, you find out about what happened when it all went up in flames.

BCDR, OPS, RISK

A Watershed Moment

This story highlights a few important but often overlooked pitfalls when preparing for a disaster. An unexpected failure caused ripple effects that no-one had envisioned, and that could have been remedied with proper risk analysis before the failure. Do not underestimate the effects of unlikely events or the amount of time it may take to recover!

BCDR, COMM, SCOPE, RISK, TRUST

Stuff Happens and Recovery Matters

Everyone has mission critical workloads, but when those workloads are for a hospital network they can be the difference between life and death. The basement datacenter in a hospital goes into cardiac arrest after a simple mistake occurs during a planned upgrade, but thankfully patient care remained unaffected. The customer knows best, except when they do not, and two IT professionals lose their weekend in a manic race to restore services before they are missed.

$, ANALYSIS, COMM, NETWORK, SCOPE, STORAGE, TIME, TRUST

Every Step Counts…

The customer was a hospital with limited availability to implement the project. The issues include people, process, and profitability of a consulting project with missing project pieces, skipped steps, and a lack of coordination, This on-premise greenfield deployment story also applies to other on-premise or cloud implementations.

ANALYSIS, BCDR, CHANGE, SCOPE, SUPPORT, TIME

The Longest Work Weekend

Although the impact was not major, the failure resulted in a very long working weekend; all as a result of an upgrade that went wrong. Lack of research and missed dependencies are some of the challenges faced.

ANALYSIS, AVAIL, BCDR, RCA, STORAGE

Do Not Neglect the Conceptual Layer

An architect's view of a support escalation where the customer's environment suffered as a result of both natural growth and conceptual design issues. It is critical to follow an enterprise architecture methodology to properly understand problems at both a business and technical level, and achieve the desired outcomes to resolve the escalation in a timely manner and with a long term solution that mitigates the risk of future business impact such as downtime or data loss.

BCDR, RCA, RISK, SCOPE, TIME, WAR

Architecting for a War Zone

This story is unique in that it describes designing a country-wide BCDR solution in a war zone. The focus is on the challenges faced and how they were overcome while dealing with an especially risky environment that impacted the scope of the project, and the time to complete it.

ANALYSIS, CHANGE, POLITICS, RISK, SUPPORT, TRUST, WAR

What is Mission Critical

Have you ever thought about what your mission-critical applications are doing to contribute to the mission of the business? Do you even know what the business mission is? This story takes you on a journey from business to mission critical and will change the way you look at mission critical-applications.

COMM, EUC, POLITICS, RCA, SCOPE, STAKEHOLDER

Absent Stakeholders and Missing Requirements

Virtual Desktop Infrastructure projects can be very complex, especially in large organizations. Can a complex project survive and still meet its original goals when key stakeholders are not invited to participate?

ANALYSIS, CHANGE, COMM, PERSP, RISK, SALES, SCOPE, TIME

How to Win Big in Uncertainty

An architect's eventful adventure while delivering IT-powered business transformation, with a variety of valuable life lessons.

COMM, RCA, SCOPE, TIME, TRUST

Follow the Process: It is Really Simple

Executing your plan while following well established processes brings you closer to success. Not following the process almost turns this project into a FAIL.

COMM, NETWORK, TRUST

A Case of NICs on vSphere

Compatibility lists exist for a reason. Just because something was compatible with the last version does not mean it is still supported in the latest product. Always check the compatibility or interoperability matrix yourself!

AUTO, COMM, SCOPE, STAKEHOLDER, TIME

Know Your Audience

Sometimes, it is not just about the technology. Sometimes, it is all about the who and why. We learned this the hard way, but managed to turn the project around and complete it successfully.

COMM, PERSP, TRUST

Self-Absorbed Summer Camp Server

Overcoming a fear of presenting at a summer camp for disabled children helped the contributor learn to teach highly technical students and present to executives. Facilitating a learning environment requires listening to an audience, making the presentation about them, and having fun. Entertaining on stage at camp opened up communication skills to create a learning environment for all kinds of audiences, both technical and non-technical.

BCDR, RISK, ROBO, SEC

Ransomware Recovery

Ransomware poses a significant threat to all IT organizations. Remediation from such attacks often requires the full execution of a company's disaster recovery plan. This story explores a large multi-national corporation's experience from initial infection to full remediation, highlighting unforeseen vulnerabilities and lessons learned.

ANALYSIS, EUC, PERSP, RISK, SCOPE

One Redundant Desktop

The client needs redundant virtual desktops for all of their sites, and their engineers need GPUs. Will this work? A sales engineer discovers what is possible from acceptance testing to business outcomes with virtual desktops.

COMM, EUC, RISK, SCOPE

A Bad Assumption and Neglected Diligence

Bad assumptions can seriously impact a project. This story describes a real-life scenario that turned the seemingly successful delivery of a VDI platform into a serious challenge, and examines how the issues could have been avoided.

$, ANALYSIS, BCDR, RISK, STORAGE, SUPPORT, TRUST

Support Matters

A storage refresh project failed due to not understanding the application stack, penny pinching, abysmally poor vendor support, and weak IT Service Management. The long-term consequences were a failed regulatory audit, and a fired CIO.

ANALYSIS, COMM, PERSP, POLITICS, SKILL

Best Practices Are There for a Reason

Best practices are not always well understood or followed. Sometimes this is due to project team members having different skill levels and perspectives, but it's often because "this is how we have always done it."

ANALYSIS, AUTO, COMM, PERSP, SCOPE

POC Stands for Production, Operation, and (scope) Creep

An automation project for a Fortune 100 company started as a Proof of Concept, but turned into a major example of scope creep. When things are out of your control, just put in your 110% and you still might win!

COMM, CHANGE, EUC, PERSP, TIME

Smell the Roses

This is a story that may seem all too familiar to many of us. A journey about dedication to the craft and getting lost in the passion of the work, all the while forgetting about what matters most, you. Know when to call it quits for the day, and understand the impact that your actions may have for everyone around you.

$, ANALYSIS, COMM, OPS, PERSP, SCOPE, SKILL

The Digital Transformation Journey to the Cloud

We live in a hybrid-multi-cloud world, but the cloud is not a panacea. This is a story about digital transformation and provides insight into some things to consider on your cloud journey.

COMM, PERSP, SKILL, TIME

Building Bridges to Success

You want to progress? You strive for promotion? Technical knowledge will help you achieve that, but there are other crucial factors that are often overlooked or neglected. This story relates one architect's experience as he progressed up the career ladder.

Please Share Your Feedback

We value your feedback! Please tell us what we are doing well, point out areas that need improvement, and share with us ideas for new content that would benefit aspiring and practicing infrastructure design architects.

If there are other topics that you would like to see covered in the IT Architect Series, please let us know. We are interested in material tied to infrastructure design such as software-defined networking, software-defined storage, security, applications, AI, IoT, autonomous systems, operations, and cloud.

When you share your feedback, please include this book's title, along with your name, e-mail address, and phone number. We will carefully review your comments but may not always be able to provide a direct response to all submissions. Thank you for sharing with us!

We look forward to working with both current and new contributors to continue the series. If you have an interesting story with lessons learned that you would like to share, please let us know. Reach out via Twitter to John Arrasjid @vcdx001 or Mark Gabryjelski @MarkGabbs.

COMM, OPS, SUPPORT

Editor's Preface

As I reviewed the stories in this book I realized that many of the lessons learned by IT architects parallel many of my own lessons learned over a 47-year career in technology. I would like to share a few short stories from the pre-virtualization days about my journey and experiences as a datacenter manager, usability engineer, and technical writer.

Early Disaster Recovery

My father was an early employee at IBM. When I was only 9-months old a pot of boiling coffee accidently fell on me causing third-degree burns, and I was not expected to live. IBM's founding CEO, Thomas Watson, heard that one of his employee's children had been critically injured and had a helicopter rush me from upstate N.Y. to a burn center in NYC. I survived, and my parents never received a bill for any of the medical care! (Can you imagine this happening in a modern corporation?!) In a sense, I owe everything to technology.

Lessons learned: Something about risk identification and mitigation, rapidly escalating critical issues to an appropriate level of support, and supporting your employees to earn lifelong gratitude and loyalty....

Magic

While working on my Master's degree in Research Psychology I was the Teacher's Assistant who ran the biofeedback lab at a major university. The day before we were to run an experiment a friend and I were struggling to get an analog/digital interface working between an EKG and an Apple II. We needed parts but it was late and there was no way to get them.

After a while we started playing with the software and many hours later we had successfully simulated the action of some electronic components and conditioned the signal so that we could run our experiment. Software (symbolic representations) can actually replace physical components! It was a revelation—this was real magic and we did not even have to chant and throw chicken feathers at it!

This experience gave me a deep appreciation for technology and its possibilities. We eventually built a 4-channel A/D plug-in card for the Apple II and dreamed about productizing it, but Apple decided no more open bus and started shipping Macs.

Lessons learned: Work with your vendors and watch your competitors for technology changes that might impact your product or service; otherwise, your plan might get unexpectedly innovated out of existence. When blocked, look for creative solutions. And something not obvious in the early 1980s but well understood by IT architects today: software can replace or augment hardware.

A Square Peg in a Round Hole

I was the Operations Manager at a Silicon Valley minicomputer datacenter that catered to trucking companies. Billing and rating clerks at the main office of our largest customer could not get access to computer systems and sat idle while work piled up. Loads could not be picked up or delivered until the paperwork was ready and hundreds of trucks were affected. We tried swapping private lines, routers, and even port multiplexor boards, all to no avail.

Finally, we asked them to use their backup 300-baud acoustic couplers to connect, but they could not get them to work. We walked through the process of setting up a coupler with their lead clerk and after a while he said "it just does not fit." Turned out that the phone company had come by and replaced all of their phone handsets with ones that had a square ear- and mouth-pieces that did not fit in the round receptacles on the acoustic couplers. This was literally a square peg in a round hole problem! We could not fix it then, but their office was only 30-miles away so we invited them to our datacenter to use our workstations and complete their work. Our customer was grateful and this was the basis for years of good relations.

Lessons learned: A non-technical person faced with a technical problem can become so uncertain and confused that basic logic fails. Train users on backup equipment. Track changes in your environment. Going the extra mile builds good customer relationships, and good relationships make everything easier.

A Haunting

While working as an IT manager in an 80-minicomputer datacenter at a large corporation an unusual labor problem occurred. Most of the computer operators on the evening shift were first-generation Americans or immigrants from a largely Catholic country. One of the best-liked operators was responsible for machines on a floor away from the main area, and while on vacation in his home country he suffered a fatal heart attack. The other operators feared that his spirit was restless and refused to work on the floor where he had worked! Managers threatened disciplinary action, operators were "written up," and the most vocal operator was even told he could be suspended. The operators filed union grievances and still refused to work in that area. Finally, an unusually sensible manager called the deceased operator's local priest who came to the datacenter to say a prayer and sprinkle some holy water. Problem solved!

Lessons learned: People are always an important part of the equation. Be aware of and respect cultural differences. An authoritarian approach might get the work done, but it causes division and resentment, and rarely resolves core people issues. Look for a solution that takes everyone's concerns into account and lets everyone win.

A Red Alert

Working as an Operations Analyst on mainframe IBM and Amdahl systems at a large corporation I monitored systems where outages cost >$1M per hour. Careers were made and broken depending on how long it took to resolve an outage, and if you missed or actually caused a problem you were doomed.

Critical alerts scrolled by in red text on our monitors, and I could not read the messages because I am completely red/green colorblind (about 8% of males have this deficiency though it varies by region and race). Fortunately, when I saw a reddish smudge go by I was usually able to query the system to determine the problem, but I sometimes had to ask a colleague to read the alerts for me.

There was also a wall of IBM and Amdahl documentation, but no-one had time to find what they needed when an outage occurred. I pulled information out of those documents and started writing site-specific runbooks and troubleshooting guides that other analysts valued and copied. It was the start of my technical writing career....

Lessons learned: Be aware that many people are red/green colorblind and use colors they can see. Consider making text colors user definable. Do not use color unless it is necessary or improves the user experience, and be aware that color has different significance in different cultures. Site-specific runbooks and troubleshooting guides are essential for effective operation of a datacenter.

Reading and Best Practices

I was the documentation coordinator and lead technical writer for a massive $150M development effort for four new, emerging systems at a telecommunications research company. Four years of 12- to 18-hour days including many weekends, no kidding!

After sending some operations documentation out to customer companies for review we got feedback that it read like university-level material and was too difficult for the operators who had to use it. We discovered that some customer companies had a best practice that documentation should be written at a 10th-grade reading level, so we licensed a program that flagged words and phrases that were above a 10th-grade level and revised the documentation to fit the audience. Nothing we wrote could reduce the complexity of the systems we were developing, but operators only needed procedures and checklists associated with performing their jobs and did not care about conceptual or design material.

At this time, I also took an Information Mapping course (my introduction to structured writing), and learned best practices for writing all kinds of documentation. I shared this knowledge with the other writers and our documentation became a lot more consistent and concise.

Lessons learned: Know your audience. Be aware of best practices that apply for your audience or environment. Leverage technology (such as the reading-level check program) and best practices to achieve your goal. Share knowledge with your colleagues. Personally, this project stretched me beyond all limits, but somehow I grew and even excelled. I was recognized for achieving an almost impossible task and most importantly, I learned what I was capable of and proved myself to my self.

An Unusable Interface

As a usability engineer I designed and ran iterative, think-aloud tests for installation and installation documentation for a major Unix release. Three experienced Unix administrators had failed to successfully install and configure the OS per the task scenarios, especially from the network, and I had been begging the development manager to observe a test session.

The manager finally visited as I was about to run a test with a university Unix administrator who managed over 10k accounts, and after watching for a few minutes he called his entire team to attend the session. The team crammed into my little observation area and seemed shocked as they watched the administrator repeatedly fail. The interface (and documentation) was rewritten soon after the session.

Lessons learned: It does not matter how good the software is if the human-computer interface is confusing or counter-intuitive—it must be usable. Observe users working in their normal work environment, if possible. Always test your work product with real users. Real users will break things you thought were bulletproof in a matter of minutes.

In Conclusion

Though I came to my lessons learned by a different path, many of them are echoed by the architects in their stories. Foundational best practices in technical writing require analyzing and knowing your audience, and communicating at their level. Usability engineering demands an understanding of how people interact with technology, and you must test with real users. And datacenter management requires both technical knowledge and soft skills. Some of the most basic principles of technical writing, usability engineering, and datacenter management are shared by IT architects and are essential to their work.

I enjoyed the variety of experiences and learned a lot from the stories in this book. I recognized similarities to my own experiences, gained some insights, and a few times almost shouted out loud “No, no, do not do that!” As you read these stories I hope you benefit from the experiences and lessons learned, and avoid the pitfalls your colleagues encountered. To quote an old adage: “Those who do not learn from the lessons of history are doomed to repeat them.”

Matthew Wood
Editor-in-Chief

Location, Location, Location

While working with customers from many industries, I discovered some surprising choices related to facilities. These choices have to do with how the facility is built and where the datacenter is located.

In this case there was a specific aspect to the facilities that was puzzling, especially as I learned more about the choices and reasons for the choices. This had to do with the aspects of liquids in and around a datacenter.

$$f(\text{liquids, datacenter}) = \text{disaster}$$

The Project

For my customer, ITAR, I was the lead architect focused on review and recommendations for their disaster preparedness. ITAR had built out their infrastructure using both old and new facilities. New facilities were designed by building architects, factoring input from the ITAR IT organization. Old facilities were retrofitted for use.

The building under review had three levels and included a datacenter, offices, conference rooms, and a recreation room. This building was one of the older facilities that had to be retrofitted to fit ITAR's needs.

- ITAR was able to reuse office space on the third and fourth floors. Electrical and networking were upgraded on these floors to meet the needs of the employees occupying this area.
- ITAR chose to keep the recreation center in its existing location on the second floor. This area was brought up to current building code, but this effort required no specific technical changes other than updating some electric outlets, installation of a sprinkler system on the entire floor, and installation of a new smoke detection system.

- When deciding on where to place the datacenter, they chose the first floor instead of the basement. This was due to some challenges on rebuilding the basement for a datacenter, including humidity that could impact the systems.

As I reviewed the environment I learned that the existing liquid pipes within the building were kept as is, in their original locations. They had separate pipes for clean water and wastewater use. The clean water pipes were white and the wastewater pipes were gray. All existing pipes were inspected and met current regulations. These pipes were on every floor in the building, from basement to the fourth floor.

When I inspected the datacenter room, I found both white and grey pipes running along the ceiling and branching into different areas. I also noticed blue pipes, but only on this floor, and only over a section of the datacenter. It turned out the blue pipes were used for water circulation for the pool on the second floor. In my risk assessment, the liquid pipes in the datacenter location were the highest risk areas I identified.

The client project manager, Joe, felt that I had misjudged the risk as they had been using the datacenter without issue for years without signs of leaks or other concerns. However, the customer directed me to describe the risks in my assessment, and I did so as follows:

> "Upon inspection of the physical elements of the datacenter environment, we have identified liquid hazards that pose the risk of damage to the servers and other devices in the datacenter room. Of particular risk is that these pipes are hanging from the ceiling, and over the server racks. Mitigation is recommended. This would require careful consideration as the datacenter was built without relocating the pipes. The recommendation is to work with a facilities architect and a team of specialists to determine the safest approach to move the pipes without impacting the underlying datacenter equipment."

As a design for relocating the pipes was out of scope for this risk assessment, there was additional information about potential options. The risk assessment was presented and reviewed. The customer signed off that the assessment was complete and I moved on to other projects.

The Failure

Later that year there was an exceptionally cold winter. One weekend there was an ice storm that caused power outages across the area, including the datacenter location. Power was required to run the datacenter equipment, but was also required for the building's heating. The UPS systems kept the computer systems running, but the heating had no backup power solution. This resulted in several frozen pipes bursting and soaking server, networking, and storage equipment, which were by then off as the UPS batteries were exhausted and the power was still out. No generator was available to provide another backup source of power, and due to the weather, no staff were present at the facility on the weekend.

How It Impacted My Customer

ITAR employees returned to work on Monday and the power returned around 9 a.m. The IT team evaluated the outage and planned to bring the servers back online, but this was not possible. Burst pipes had leaked on the server, networking, and storage equipment! The water destroyed equipment, and left a layer of water under the raised floor, making for a potentially electrifying experience if safety precautions were not met.

ITAR had to deal with the electrical hazards with liquids present. Beyond the risk of electrocution to team members working on recovery, they were thankful that the gray pipes had not burst, or there would have been additional safety issues with wastewater.

The recovery process took approximately one week to address the damaged pipes and removal of water. Millions of dollars of soaked equipment had to be scrapped and replaced.

What Could I Have Done Differently?

Although out of scope, I should have added details on the potential risk outcomes and recommended at least one approach that the ITAR team could tackle. The ITAR team would require specialists to relocate the liquid pipes to eliminate the risk. These specialists would include datacenter architects, plumbers, electricians, and facilities experts to plan out an effective way to remove the risk, or relocate the datacenter.

This particular site was only 10% virtualized. I would recommend increasing the level of virtualization to make it easier to move systems if the base hardware is damaged or destroyed.

What Did I Learn?

I learned that the location of equipment and facilities resources is essential for availability and recovery.

The pipes should have been relocated before building the datacenter, but this is not always possible. The following are some of the options that could be considered in a follow-on project with the customer to determine what would work best for ITAR. Some of these options may be combined to provide a better solution.

Option #1: Liquid-carrying pipes should be removed from the datacenter room.

Option #2: Relocate the datacenter systems to another facility or area of the building where there is no risk from liquids.

Option #3: If pipes must remain in the room due to budget, then additional shielding of the pipes is recommended, with additional ways to divert liquids in the event of a similar disaster. An example of this type of diversion of water is with a server umbrella, called a *shell* that sits over the server racks. An example comes from a company called Turtle Shell Industries (turtleshellproducts.com).

Option #4: Upgrade all racks to NEMA 12-rated enclosures. This provides limited water protection, but is not 100% waterproof.

Option #5: Virtualize more of the server equipment to simplify recovery, supporting the ability to relocate the virtual machines in advance of a predicted disaster. This can also simplify the recovery process of systems onto alternative hardware, something that virtualization allows. Today, this level of virtualization can be extended to cloud solutions for recovery.

In addition to deciding on one or more of these options, the heating and cooling system within the building should be added to the backup power equipment (UPS and generator) for the building.

In conclusion, the risk identified in my assessment could have been easily mitigated in advance of the datacenter buildout, but was significantly more challenging after the datacenter was built. The cost to make a change after the full buildout of the datacenter would be significantly higher than if planned in advance. Addressing risk after a disaster is never the best option.

Careful planning of the architecture, and taking a more realistic look at the risks of every decision, can prevent these types of disasters from occurring. In design we consider people, process, and things (technology).

In this situation, the disaster was a result of a combination of failures in the following areas.

- ITAR accepted the risk of liquids flowing directly over the datacenter equipment, risking damage to the hardware and flooding of the under-floor space that contained cabling and power.
- The process accepted the reduced budget without reviewing the risks, forcing existing pipes to be in the highest risk location for the company.
- The technology considerations did not emphasize the value of virtualization to increase the ease of server relocation and/or recovery.

In the world of datacenter design, just as in real estate, we need to think “location, location, location” when making our choice in datacenter placement!

Prerequisites and Project Plans Matter

This is a fun little story in hindsight, but only in hindsight. It was a horrible experience for me and for my team, and even more so for the customer.

It started out well...planning, researching, validating, and testing, followed by acceptance of the defined process. We did everything that anyone embarking on an infrastructure upgrade would do to avoid problems. Despite this, the project went wrong, very wrong, and I believe it was my fault. Why? Let me start at the beginning....

The Project

We were planning a VMware vSphere upgrade to version 5.5 for a customer. Days of preparations went into this upgrade, including:

- The VMware Hardware Compatibility List (HCL) was reviewed to verify that servers would be compatible with the new release.
- The firmware on the VMware ESXi servers was upgraded to latest versions.
- Vendor-appropriate ESXi ISOs were prepared to support a rebuild of ESXi servers (instead of an upgrade in place).
- The latest version of VMware vCenter 5.5 was downloaded, and all of the licenses on the customer's VMware portal were upgraded from 4.x to 5.x vSphere license keys.
- We planned for the Veeam Backup & Replication servers that would be deployed as part of the solution.

During a project planning meeting, we also planned for a few new host IP addresses and corresponding DNS entries. We were going to stand up a net-new vCenter (appliance) and we had to create a new DNS entry for this because it would be deployed while the existing vCenter was still managing the vSphere 4.x environment. The customer took an action item to get the new entries put into DNS before starting the project.

The Failure

We had a final project planning meeting before we were to start the deployment of the new vCenter and upgrade (rebuild) of ESXi hosts. Then, vSphere 6.0 was released four days before project work was to begin.

Version Change

Upon hearing that the new version of vSphere had been released, the customer wanted to change the upgrade to vSphere 6.0. They did not want to upgrade to something that was "already out of date." I argued that this was new software and that there might be some risk in deploying a release that has no proven track record. The customer responded that they did not want to upgrade to vSphere 5.5 and then later have to upgrade to vSphere 6.0. Though I understood and acknowledged their position, I still believed that running new software had risks. However, as a result of the discussion a change control was submitted to upgrade to vSphere 6.0 instead of vSphere 5.5.

Prerequisites Failure

After arriving onsite and getting set up for a day of deployment and configuration, we ran through the installation checklists that we had created for this project. The first step in my checklists is always DNS validation: ping each host by IP, by hostname, by FQDN, and perform an nslookup to make sure reverse DNS is functioning. Responses were not expected or received; this was just a way to validate that the new DNS entries had been made and name resolution was in place.

The customer had assured me that DNS would be set up. I noted that there was no response from a ping by hostname or FQDN, and that nslookup was not returning any results. The customer replied, “Oh yeah, I still need to do that.”

OK, only a handful of new DNS entries were required so a 10-30 minute delay was no big deal. Then the customer asked, “Do you know how to add an entry into BIND?”

Alright, I thought…, this may not be the person who usually manages DNS, so I helped get the new entries into the zone config files. I tested name resolution again and it was still not working. I flushed the DNS cache and tried again. Still nothing…. I noted to the customer that name resolution was still failing and the customer replied, “Oops…forgot to run that script.”

I asked about the script and the customer stated, “Oh, well DNS replication is broken, so we have a script that copies all the files to all the other DNS servers every time we add records to DNS.”

I should have stopped everything at this point, but I did not want to upset my customer by harping on the issue. They ran their script to replicate DNS and name resolution finally started working.

Schedule Change

We deployed the new virtual machine for the VMware vCenter 6.0 appliance, and then deployed the appliance. The environment was up and running, and ready to take over the ESXi hosts.

We started moving ESXi hosts from the old vCenter to the newly deployed vCenter 6.0. Our process was to put a host into maintenance mode, remove it from the old vCenter inventory, install a fresh installation of ESXi 6.0 (using its original hostname), and add it to the new vCenter and into the correct VMware cluster object. We followed this process for two of the six hosts in the main VMware cluster. As a result of planning and communication users expected to have their applications interrupted during the day, which gave us time to unregister some VMs from the old vCenter and register them on the new ESXi hosts being managed by the new vCenter.

The process was repeated as we migrated over all the VMs, kept rebuilding hosts, and completed the migration of this one cluster and its VMs. It seemed like we were ready to apply the patches that VMware Update Manager had already downloaded for vSphere 6.0. Then, the customer stated that my focus should change to moving the rest of the ESXi hosts between vCenter servers. He wanted to finish the work today, rather than as scheduled over the next week!

This was a significant change to the project plan. Even so, there was still plenty of time to move all of the other ESXi clusters, and we always want to make the customer happy, right? While moving the hosts, we started preparing the new backup jobs for VMs. Fast forward to the end of a long day, and we were done. All the hosts were moved well ahead of schedule, and the backup jobs were running successfully against the new vCenter Server.

SQL Server Corruption

The next morning I was awakened by the phone ringing, and the first words I heard from the customer were, “Our main SQL server is corrupt.” The entire set of databases on this server was no longer valid, and needed to be restored from backup. Not the best way to start the day....

The customer looked at the backup server, saw no errors in the backup job from the previous night, and attempted to restore all of the databases. The restore job completed successfully, but the databases were still corrupted. Not good.... They went back an additional day, and restored a full VM copy of the database server from two days previous (the last backup from the old vCenter). This was sent to the new vCenter server as a net new VM so we could analyze the SQL server. This went well, and they were soon back up and running.

Unfortunately, they had lost a day of data, and a lot of effort had to be put into data entry to make up for the loss. This was not expected or planned for, and was very manual process. Plus, it had taken nearly a full day to get the SQL server back, so a second day was lost.

The following morning started exactly the same way as the previous day (this is day 2 after the upgrade). The SQL server was corrupt again! They had already started restoring from the previous night's backup and the restore was nearly done. Meanwhile, I went to see the customer to try to work out what was going on. During my drive, they called me and told me that the restored SQL server was still corrupt, and they would again have to restore the SQL server from the old backup. That was not good as it would result in a two-day old SQL database, require lots of manual entries and updates, and we still did not know why the SQL server was corrupted.

Finally, the SQL server was up and running and we began trying to find the problem. After a few hours, we identified the time frame when the SQL server became corrupt. The only thing that we could correlate to that time frame was that backups were occurring. Those timelines crossed perfectly, so we started looking at backups.

Reviewing the backup logs produced nothing. The VMware CBT function was enabled, VSS was enabled, and application-consistent snapshots were taken. The backup logs and the VMware logs were clean. It looked like the backup software was causing the SQL server to corrupt its data, but that is not how it works! CBT keeps track of changed blocks. The first backup of the SQL server using the new vCenter on this new ESXi host had to be a full backup as it was technically a new VM, even though we had migrated it. With a completely new vCenter server, all VMs are new because the MoRefID (Managed Object Reference ID) is not moved. The Veeam server would not know which VM was which, so all VMs would be treated as a new VM, not just the SQL server.

I had not seen this problem before so I called the backup vendor for support. The vendor was phenomenally good and provided constant phone support for a month until the issue was resolved.

An Unknown Known Issue

Long story short.... The initial GA release of vSphere 6.0 shipped with a CBT bug (discovered about three weeks after release) that affected certain workloads, such as SQL. If I had pushed back on using the latest version of vSphere none of this would have happened as Version 5.5 of vSphere did not have the CBT bug. I would have had to later perform another upgrade to get to vSphere 6.0, but in hindsight, this would have been a better approach.

How It Impacted My Customer

This brought down production for the customer. Given that all workflows went through the SQL server affected by the bug there was a major impact to the operation of the organization. The outage required four weeks of effort from their team and my team to resolve this issue, only to find out it was a known bug.

What Could I Have Done Differently?

There are several key takeaways from this engagement:

- Prerequisites: I should have stopped the project when the prerequisites were not met, and offered to help correctly resolve the issue. They were struggling with DNS and I should have offered more assistance in this area of their infrastructure (that I needed to rely on). When I did offer help, they responded that they had it under control.

  I should not have accepted their assurance, nor accepted the state of DNS in their environment. I should have halted the project, written up a change control, and gotten DNS fixed. My change control request could have been denied, but at least I would have called out that this issue needed to be addressed, and the risk it posed to the overall infrastructure.

  I should also have reviewed the known issues within the environment before starting.

- Deployment: I should not have allowed a customer to pressure me with an artificial timeline and should not have ignored my own process documentation. If I had installed the planned version of ESXi to the servers rather than hurrying to meet their deadline and desire to be on the latest software version, the problem would have been avoided. If I had not moved all of the other clusters during the first day, and instead had migrated them the following week as planned, the issue would not have occurred as the SQL server was on the second set of ESXi hosts migrated.
- Push back: Yes, with the prerequisites and deployment (meow). Building a solution on a net new version of software that was released only days earlier, to accommodate a customer request, poses a risk. Though I called this out, I should have been adamant about removing risk from the customer's infrastructure as they did not have the ability or requirement to take on that risk. When pushing back it is important to not be confrontational. I would look at ways to educate the customer so that they fully understand the risk and reasons for my recommendation, and can transfer their knowledge to future projects.

What Did I Learn?

When you identify problems in a customer's environment and see them struggling to work through them, offer them help. Sometimes this requires additional time, cost, and a project change order. Create the change order outlining risk, cost, and benefit, and submit it to the customer. Let the customer be the one to reject the change. Otherwise, it may come back to haunt you later, as it did in this case.

It is my job as an architect to stop a project when things are going wrong, identify the issues, and work to resolve them. I failed to do that in this case. I should have stopped the project when it was discovered that DNS was not working. If DNS does not work properly, nothing works!

Just because your primary customer contact wants to meet a deadline does not mean you need to take on additional risk to achieve it. I understand, Mr. Customer, that you want to go on vacation next week, and that this delay will mean coming back from vacation while the project is still in progress, but would you rather cancel your vacation to resolve outages that could easily have been avoided?

When you take on a customer's project you become part of their team. I create installation and validation documents, procedures, and checklists to avoid problems. Do not skip basic checks and balances prior to installation even if the primary customer contact states that their required preparation is complete. Something as minor as a typo in DNS could affect everything else you are building for them. Verify that prerequisites validation is done, and double-check it if needed.

Make sure you investigate and validate each part of the solution. Do not go forward without performing your due diligence.

An Architect's VDI aPOCalypse

I was engaged in a head-to-head Virtual Desktop Infrastructure (VDI) proof of concept (POC) to help a large company re-platform their desktops into VDI before moving into their new, soon to open headquarters building. I was alone on the project, and our competitor had a team of several people who started weeks before I did.

The Project

The first few steps were straightforward: build the infrastructure, stand up the gold image they gave me, and add a few applications to it. I was significantly ahead of schedule and quickly moved forward with the rollout phase. I used a typical trickle rollout strategy. Working with the customer's team, we selected a few representative users in the department and built gold images and application packages. We sent the help desk team to work with the users. Then, we used a script to copy the user's files into a file share, and convert their desktop into a rugged thin client.

The company's move deadline was aggressive. I worked day and night. During the day, I managed the rollout, handled escalations, and held meetings with departments and groups to understand use cases. After the rollouts stopped for the day, I stayed late at the office working on new application layers, making gold image tweaks, and more. I told myself that I did not have time to write a design document, and it was true, and honestly, it seemed like everything was working at the time.

The two competing POC teams shared office space with the new HQ building consultants who ordered all the furniture, got the walls painted, and so on. Looking back, it might not have been the best idea to put us literally face-to-face with a competitor in a winner takes all deal. Anyway, I repeatedly put in 16 hours at the office, headed to the hotel, ordered another Sloppy Joe and French fries (and a DoubleTree cookie-crust cheesecake) from room service, passed out, and did the whole thing again the next day. (I think I gained 10 pounds on this project.)

The Failure

The first issues arose in the call center group. The call center group dealt with financial documents, and they all had scanners on their desks. They depended on a suboptimal Microsoft Internet Explorer plus ActiveX application, and scanned documents for their line of business. I heard reports of trouble from call center users unable to do their jobs. You would think a large group with a lot of identical users would be an easy rollout—if it worked for one user in the group, it should work for all, right? Looking into it, I discovered that the call center users and their desktops were wildly divergent. Rather than the clean environment I had been promised and assumed was in place, users and their desktops were packed in all manner of Active Directory Organizational Units (OUs), inheriting a crazy quilt of group policy driving the Internet Explorer settings to make that app work. I had not done a current state analysis and just relied on the data I was given about the department, and I had not investigated the internals of the app.

An attempt to unify all of the users into one OU, and all of the desktops into another OU, was a disaster. We did not have accurate user lists, and to make it worse the chief Active Directory administrator left without warning on a long vacation. This forced me to start over working with a junior administrator.

Then another problem occurred! The end users could not consistently scan. While my competitor seemed to have no trouble with this, I was stuck in a quagmire. I eventually identified the following issues:

- There was supposed to be a standard scanner purchased for all users, but the procurement group had bought some based on lowest cost. They had assembled a fleet of scanners from several different manufacturers with a variety of different models.

- The VDI vendor I was using relies on a third-party, white-labelled scanner redirection library. Opening a case with the vendor, they determined the new version of the VDI software, which I had deployed despite its having been released only a few weeks previously, had some bugs. They got me a hotfix but it did not help.

Eventually, my management directed me to focus on writing a design document, while our competitor continued to brute-force their way through the project with an army of poorly skilled personnel. We lost the deal. I wasted a lot of time and expenses on the project, and ended up working over a holiday due to a DR test.

How It Impacted My Customer

Both my POC and the competitor's POC were unsuccessful. The competitor ran into issues similar to mine, and failed even though they had more time and resources. Eventually, the customer terminated the VDI project and went back to physical desktops. We wasted the call center users' time fighting issues, and failed to help the customer move from desktops to VDI. This was a POC apocalypse, or an aPOCaplypse, as I titled this story.

What Could I Have Done Differently?

Although there are many things I would do differently, the following are at the top of my list:

- Design Document: This is essential. Developing a design document would have made a significant difference in outcomes for both POCs. Even a basic design document would have provided a structured and planned approach for the POC deployment and testing.
- Statement of Work (SOW): Have a complete SOW with properly defined deliverables, along with a test plan that maps test use cases back to requirements. In this case success criteria were not properly defined.

- Current state analysis: Do not take the customer's word for the current state. They do not intend to lie or mislead you, but in large underfunded environments, especially if there are multiple outsourcing teams involved, things will be missed and handoffs will fail.
- Risk Management: New software could be risky. With newer software, there is a risk of unknown bugs that might cause critical issues. Older software may have support challenges, and may require updates. There are advantages to running the last patch version of the last release rather than charging headlong into a new release, especially if you do not need the new features. It would be great to go into production with no technical debt, but on a tight timeline I would rather use known software and preserve the option for an upgrade (because downgrades are not always possible).
- Rollout and politics: I was only one person, and I could not hand-hold the help desk, deal with end users, and properly research, design, and think through the technical implications of every choice. My competitor had more resources, and they were local and culturally savvy. I was an outsider. More resources early in the project would have helped.

What Did I Learn?

Consider the following lessons learned from this project:

- Write architecture documentation: I missed a lot of important areas. Write a good architecture document and include design decisions, why choices were made, and descriptions of how the infrastructure will be built. Writing architecture documents helps you think through every aspect of what you are doing end to end.

  When you write, you inevitably read reference material. Had I done so, I would have caught several obvious mistakes. I would have realized that I had misremembered how important pieces worked and would have avoided false leads when I ran into problems. Looking back on it years later, if the project had continued, I would almost certainly have run into other problems caused by some bad technical decisions I made though I thought I knew how things worked.

- Call for help: I should have realized that I needed more help after I ran into trouble and brought it in sooner. By the time the project was a shambles, it was too late. Always keep the project manager and the management chain up to date with the status so there are no surprises.
- Conservative approach: Third-party dependencies in off-the-shelf software strike me as especially risky, because when you are calling support and getting engineering help there is stuff going on behind the curtains that you cannot see. The vendor may not have the source code and may not be able to figure out what is wrong with it in a timely manner. Patches and hotfixes are practically guaranteed to arrive after they are needed, and the documentation you get on how that third-party component works is rarely good enough. It is not always possible to avoid software that has dependencies, but taking a conservative approach and staying with old and known software, versus new and unknown software, can avoid a lot of problems.

Architecture matters, even for a POC!

A Murphy's Law Datacenter Migration

Murphy's Law does exist!

This was a rushed and disorganized project, with poor planning, preparation, and execution. Throw in a last-minute vendor change, unsupported storage adapters, untested deployment scripts, and a knowledge gap, and everything that could go wrong did go wrong....

The Project

My customer needed to complete a datacenter migration and hardware refresh by the end of the year. The contract for their datacenter was expiring, and their hardware was either end-of-life (EOL) or quickly approaching EOL. Their long-term objective was to create a private Software Defined Datacenter (SDDC). The entirely new datacenter was an opportunity to start from scratch with a clean slate.

A valued partner planned do the professional services work alongside the customer from start to finish, and had the boots on the ground to do the job.

The Failure

There were many issues and failures during this project.

POC Failures

A total of three Hyper-Converged Infrastructure (HCI) solutions were tested during a brief POC phase in the early half of the year. The customer explored the possibility of moving everything into a VMware Cloud on Amazon Web Services, but due to maturity concerns with the solution they decided to stay with an on-premises HCI solution. I got the impression that they had their sights on a specific solution for some time, decided to vet some other solutions as part of due diligence, and then provide their leadership with a ranking and an estimated cost for each solution.

From my perspective, this phase was rushed and not properly vetted.

A lot of processes and scenarios were overlooked during the POC. It was limited to deploying VMs from scratch, cloning VMs, observing disk capacity, and minimal performance testing narrowly focused only on capacity. There was no runbook used by the customer or partner to make sure that they did everything possible to properly test these platforms. There should have been a validation runbook where observations were documented for various testing scenarios such as high availability during a planned or unplanned host outage, or to assess the impact to cluster resource capacity if one or more hosts are offline for a long time. This was entirely overlooked.

Planning Failures

Only one architecture planning session took place in the early stages of the project. The infrastructure team was so confident in their prior success that they felt additional reviews or additional planning sessions were not warranted given an already shortened timeline. A rough outline was drawn up alongside a basic workbook outlining tasks, roles and responsibilities. That was all, and the customer and partner signed off on this plan. They took everything they did in the legacy datacenter and applied it to the new datacenter. This approach completely contradicted the customer's original intention of starting with a clean slate and setting up a new SDDC.

Vendor Change

By late spring, there was a new sense of urgency. At the last minute, the executive team overturned the hardware vendor of choice based on another vendor's promise to get the physical hardware delivered and installed quickly. The original vendor had made a similar promise but needed two additional weeks for procurement to get the equipment. The decision to use the new hardware platform vendor was made to save two weeks runway time and was not based on any technical validation. This was entirely a "dollars and cents" move with an expectation that everyone would somehow just make it work without regard to consequences. Everything else completed up to this point was irrelevant. You can probably guess where the first problem occurred....

The hardware platform order was delayed a full month. The original plan was to have all of the equipment in house by the beginning of August, followed by a professional services engagement to assist the infrastructure team with rack, stack, and initial configurations. The first 200 nodes did not arrive until early September. This was four weeks behind schedule, all due to a promise backed by an unrealistic expectation. If it sounds too good to be true, it probably is.

100 Support Cases

Things accelerated quickly after the equipment arrived. The mindset was to hurry up and get things done as soon as possible, and Murphy's Law went into overdrive. Issues popped up left and right, including some that I had not heard about in years such as cable polarization. Then, there was a multitude of problems including power and cooling issues, faulty small form-factor pluggable transceivers (SFPs) on more than half of the shipment, internal disagreements about which TCP/IP range should be used for each purpose, incorrect DNS entries, and so on. There were over 100 support cases opened in the first six weeks of the project!

Script Issues

The infrastructure team wanted to reuse deployment scripts that had been in use for several years. These scripts were not tested during the POC phase, which would have been the perfect time to validate them. We advised everyone to test the scripts on a small subset of systems before using them against all of the new hosts, but because the team was behind schedule and extremely confident in their scripts, they decided to execute them against the entire environment.

The person who wrote the scripts and typically executed them during deployments was unavailable, but confidence was so high that they allowed one of the newer and less experienced employees to run them. Things did not work as they had hoped, and their engineer did not have the knowledge to troubleshoot the scripts, so more time was lost.

Unsupported Storage Adapters

After getting through the initial deployment issues, the VMware vSphere clusters needed to be installed and configured per the intended design, followed by virtual storage (VMware vSAN) and virtual networking (VMware NSX). This brought us to the next major issue. The bill of materials had not been validated against the vSAN compatibility list, and the storage adapters in the new hosts were not supported. They chose the cheapest option available for the server model to keep cost down on the 200 nodes as part of their last-minute decision when changing hardware platform vendors. A Return Merchandise Authorization (RMA) was issued to replace the adapters with compatible ones. This was a very time consuming and costly incident, caused by a lack of preparation and validation due to rushing this project through as fast as possible. If hardware compatibility had been validated prior to submitting the purchase order, two weeks would not have been wasted waiting on this hardware.

After the storage controllers were replaced on over 200 systems and the environment was fully configured, things settled down a bit. The environment was online by mid-November.

Knowledge Gap

The customer's infrastructure team had new team members due to an acquisition. Most people in this newer group had little knowledge or experience with the new technology, but they were responsible for supporting it after the deployment was complete. A decision was made to postpone the NSX component of the project. Not because it would take long to install, but because the infrastructure team had a major knowledge gap with the solution.

Successful Migration

The highest priority for the customer was to migrate workloads as soon as possible given that less than six weeks remained before the end of the year, including two major holidays. Customer and partner resources worked in rotations, taking turns working nights and weekends until the migration was complete. Roughly 2,500 virtual machines were slated for migration. This was the only time during the project when only very small problems occurred, and troubleshooting was allowed without filing service requests or tickets. Things went relatively well from that point on and the entire cutover was completed by the second week of February.

How It Impacted My Customer

The customer missed their deadline by five weeks and had to pay for an extra three months in the old datacenter beyond their negotiated contract. It cost them another $1.8 million dollars to remain in the legacy datacenter beyond their original contract. This could have been avoided had the proper planning and preparation time been allocated.

Lack of planning and preparation had a severe negative short- and long-term impact on my customer. They rushed everything, and in my opinion, they should have begun migration planning the year before, not within the same calendar year. This was never going to be a simple "lift and shift" migration between datacenters.

This is a very good example where "fail to plan, then plan to fail" became a reality. Minimal infrastructure planning, in conjunction with a rushed proof of concept, was a recipe for disaster. Following the planning failures with a sudden last-minute change in hardware platforms without understanding the implications or validating hardware compatibility poured gasoline on the fire. The problem that caused the issues was not discovered until the new equipment was racked and stacked and ready to go, which created another major delay.

What Could I Have Done Differently?

If I could go back and change anything regarding my role on this project, it would be to highlight the consequences of each risk and communicate it more effectively to the leadership teams. I raised awareness, but not enough for someone to officially to say, “Hey, we need to hit pause for a moment here and revisit X, Y and Z before we go any further....” If I had raised awareness to these risks more effectively, versus allowing them to be known issues, we could have saved some additional heartache.

Pause and take time to revalidate things on a project with a shortened timeline. It may seem like revalidation could waste time and negatively impact a project, but in reality, it saves time and reduces the likelihood of cost and schedule issues.

I have been part of other migrations with shortened timelines. In fact, I was one of the delivery engineers on massive datacenter migration years ago. It was extremely successful because of the amount of preparation and planning that was done each and every day, unlike this disastrous project there was a lead person on each team and they collaborated and planned together instead of having one person manage all of the leaders as a whole and orchestrate everything. I attribute the success of that project to a very good project manager. Had there been a good project manager, this project probably would have stayed on track.

We also have to accept that some factors are out of our control. For example, when the decision was made to change the core HCI platform for the entire solution, another architect and I verified the bill of materials against the Hardware Compatibility List (HCL) for vSphere and vSAN. The problem was that another individual then made a decision to change storage controllers, and did not notify us or ask us to double-check compatibility. There was an incorrect assumption made with this last-minute hardware change and it had a major negative impact to the solution and project timeline.

What Did I Learn?

I always knew and understood the risks involved in rushing projects and not being organized, but I never imagined being a part of such a project and experiencing the negative outcomes. Everything that could go wrong went wrong because of the lack of preparation and required planning. It is dangerous to assume that some of what we do on a regular basis can be skipped, for some unknown reason, when a project has a short timeframe. Somehow, we subconsciously assume that things will just work as they always have, and that is the point where we need to stop, step back, and reexamine everything. If it means spending an extra week or two to plan and prepare, do it. Raise the red flag, sound the alarm, and do whatever is necessary to bring awareness about an issue that could be a potential problem before it actually happens.

Creatures of Habit

Having spent the last two months onsite with the customer, I knew the project team very well. Even the staff at the corporate coffee shop knew me by name and knew what my favorite drink was. The coffee shop was conveniently located right next to the IT project team office. At 8 a.m., I joined the busy queue for my usual double-espresso cappuccino.

That is how I always started my day. However, later that afternoon I learned that things can change at a moment's notice. The design I was working on was almost complete when someone threw a spanner in the works.

The Project

Our customer, a large manufacturer of widgets and well-known consumer brand had started their digital transformation journey earlier that year. They had consolidated four datacenters to two at opposite ends of the country. The core networking infrastructure had already been upgraded, so it was the perfect time for me (just one year as a professional services consultant) to work on their new VMware vSphere design. On the project team, there was the customer's architect and consultants from the server and storage hardware vendor.

The Statement of Work (SOW) stated that I was to deliver a full infrastructure design for vSphere 6.5 that was to become the new platform for the customer's production workloads. The design proposed four vSphere clusters in total.

- A four-host cluster for management.
- Two sixteen-host clusters for desktop workloads. One of the clusters had GPU cards.
- A fourth cluster with twelve hosts for application servers.

The second datacenter was going to be another active site for desktop workloads, but each datacenter had the capacity to run all 3,000 desktop virtual machines in the event of a single datacenter outage.

Change

The project was going really well. This engagement really was a pleasure to work on. That is, until this conversation at the morning briefing meeting....

> "The host bus adapter (HBA) cards for the blade servers have been removed from the order. We did not have the budget for these," said the project manager.
>
> "Yep, they are not really needed anyway. The blades have 10Gb/s network adapters, more than enough bandwidth for storage," said Brian.

Brian was a storage consultant working for the hardware vendor, and was also very good friends with Steve, the project manager. Brian was not always the easiest person to work with as he often made changes without telling anyone. This was a change that could potentially turn a successful production deployment into a failure.

> "Brian, we have already done our load-testing using the physical iSCSI host bus adapters," I said. "We really need those HBAs to ensure they will get the required performance."
>
> "Can we just use the 10Gb/s adapters for iSCSI?" the project manager asked. "We have always done it that way with other customers, and never needed separate HBAs before."

I was not happy about this....

One of the customer's main concerns was storage performance. The CAD application they used had massive files that the engineering teams worked on every day. They would also run the CAD application from a VMware Horizon 7 environment. Though the servers for virtual desktops were separate from the server workloads, the storage array was shared between both environments.

> "I understand that, and it may work fine," I added. "However, we have not tested it. We are running over a hundred virtual desktops on each of those hosts, so I cannot guarantee it will perform the same without the HBAs."

The project manager suggested we discuss it offline, so we moved on to the next topic, licensing. They asked whether they could purchase the Standard edition licensing instead of Enterprise Plus. This was one unplanned change I could avoid because the Horizon 7 bundle already included vSphere for Desktop licenses equivalent to Enterprise Plus. That made Steve happy as he was able to remove some of the vSphere Enterprise Plus licenses from the quote.

As I left the meeting room, I sent a text message to the customer's lead architect. He was my source of truth, and had stipulated the performance requirements early on in the design phase. Unfortunately, he was off sick that week so I was not expecting a timely response.

With less than four weeks before going live, I felt stressed out. I considered going to Laura, the executive sponsor and CTO, but I really did not want to disturb her without first talking to the architect. To make matters worse, I had only taken one sip of my coffee before I realized they had put vanilla in it! I never put vanilla in my coffee.

The server hardware used for load-testing was due to be returned to the distributor that week. I wondered if they might be right. After all, the storage consultant has done this before so maybe I was being inflexible.

Doubt and Acquiescence

That night, after checking into the hotel, I headed straight to the lounge bar and ordered a beer. I had found a nice table next to the fireplace, a great spot to review my design and performance metrics. Perhaps, it would work without the HBAs?

Two hundred virtual desktops are persistent, so there are no boot storms to worry about. They would always be powered on, and would run on the vGPU-enabled cluster. The other desktops were not running the CAD application, but they would need to open the engineering files in a viewer app. The end users were across multiple time zones in the United States, Europe, and India, so they were not all in use at the same time. The performance testing I had done simulated a massive boot-up of all 3,000 virtual desktops and that was worst case, right? Conclusion? Yes, it will be fine.

The next morning, I saw Brian standing at the end of the line waiting for his order at the coffee shop.

> "Since when did you start drinking coffee?" I asked.
>
> "Morning!" he replied. "You have really got to try the vanilla latte. I am starting to like coffee now!"

I grumbled at that.... I could not help but wonder if he was also responsible for the terrible coffee I had the day before. I bet he told them to put vanilla in it.

> "I was looking at the performance metrics last night, Brian," I said. "I do not think changing to a software iSCSI initiator will impact the IOPS, and bandwidth should still be sufficient."
>
> "See, what did I tell you? HBA cards are overrated these days," he said.
>
> "I would still prefer that we tested it, but it seems we have no choice."
>
> "No time for that my friend," he said. "We have always done it this way, you just worry too much!"

With the customer's architect still off sick, I really did not want to bother the CTO. I decided to send another text message to tell the architect that it was all resolved and not to worry. Both the architect and the CTO had seen the results of the performance testing, and they were delighted with the speed of opening the CAD files compared to their old implementation. The virtual desktops were really fast too. This was not surprising because the disks were all flash-based and their old CAD workstations were very slow in comparison. I was satisfied. I decided to remove the HBAs from the design, but just in case, I listed it as a design constraint.

For the rest of that week, I focused on the networking design. That was the last part I needed to complete, and with the recent changes I had to include Network I/O Control to make sure the iSCSI traffic was not impacted by vMotion. I added a limit of 1Gbps for vMotion, reserved 4Gbps for iSCSI, and another 4Gbps for virtual machine traffic.

After meeting with the network team, and agreeing on the VLANs and network address space to use for the design, I left the office early to beat the traffic. The office was located close to a shopping mall, and with only two weeks before Christmas, the traffic had worsened as people rushed to buy their last-minute gifts. I could not help but be reminded of the potential bottlenecks in throughput, using the heavy traffic as an analogy to the addition of iSCSI traffic. It will be fine....

I spent the following week working from home, finishing the design documentation, and reviewing the updated project plan Steve had sent. Over the Christmas holiday week, the customer engineering team was going to take my design and implementation guide, and deploy the new infrastructure. The new solution would be live in time for everyone when they return after the holidays.

The Failure

It was Monday morning, the day after Christmas, at 8 a.m. "Yes, a double-espresso cappuccino please, no vanilla," I told the barista at the coffee shop. Brian was nowhere to be seen. Perhaps, he had realized he did not like coffee after all!

I made my way to the operations team office. It was live. My role for the week was to offer guidance and support to the customer's team as part of the agreed knowledge transfer. The virtual machines had been migrated from the old servers, and 3,000 virtual desktops were running. I had already heard from the customer's architect that India had been using the new virtual desktops since the previous week, and it was all working well. Today was the day! The local CAD engineering teams would start using the 3D-enabled desktops and new application servers.

I took a look at the Horizon Administrator console and was relieved to see 722 desktops in use. I asked the operations team if there were any support tickets opened from the India-based users, but they reported only a handful of tickets about email not working or people having the wrong printer set as the default. No performance issues!

Steve, the project manager approached me. "There is something strange going on with the virtual desktops," he said. "The CPU usage of the VDI hosts is really high—almost one hundred percent!"

The CAD engineering team, all two hundred of them, had arrived and started work for the day. The first support ticket had been logged. Slow performance. Before I could finish my coffee, there were over sixty tickets logged by that team. Something was amiss!

I sat down in front of my laptop, and logged into vCenter. Several hosts were showing alarms and the CPU usage was maxed out. I glanced up at the large monitor across the room and saw the vRealize Operations dashboard lit up like a Christmas tree. Green is good. Green and red, not so good! The CPU usage of the virtual desktops was high, but not as high as I expected. I spent the next two hours with the Operations team trying to figure out why the host performance was suffering. Then, I saw why.

HBAs

While I was troubleshooting the performance issues, the customer's architect and CTO came into the office looking concerned. I stood up, and explained.

"As you know, we did not have the budget for the additional HBA cards," I said as I walked over to the whiteboard. Drawing the same logical diagram I had used in the design, I sketched out the storage array, network switches, and hosts, along with the 10Gb/s cards.

"After looking at the performance testing results, I saw that the storage IO was read heavy for the virtual desktops, but the CAD desktops and application servers were very write heavy. Still, without HBA cards I could see the throughput was unaffected." I said, using the green marker pen to highlight the path between the storage array and network switches.

"Latency?" the CTO asked.

"That was my initial thought too," replied the architect. His arms were folded, and he had a stern look on his face. "No, it is the CPU overhead using software iSCSI."

"So…we did need the HBA cards?" said Laura, looking rather perplexed.

"Right. We did not see any overhead at all during the initial performance tests as we were using a pair of HBA cards for each host." I continued by drawing on the whiteboard, illustrating the HBA cards. "Network IO Control is handling the bandwidth, and latency is not an issue at all. However, the CPU usage for the CAD applications is high because it is handling all of those massive files. I knew this was high, but we had designed the hosts to have a peak average of around eighty percent." I sat down, and continued my explanation. "The added load of software iSCSI is just enough to max out the CPU along with the CAD workloads."

"Can we take the HBA cards from the old servers?" asked Steve, the project manager who sat opposite me.

"No, they are blade mezzanine cards," I replied. "They will fit into the other hosts, but not the ones used for CAD as they are rackmount. We need to order the HBA cards."

Just as I spoke those words, I saw Brian, the storage architect stood in the doorway. He did not say anything and I did not call him out. It was my design, and my mistake.

"How quickly can we get the cards?" Brian asked as he gestured towards Steve.

"We can get them here same day."

I left that day feeling that my mistake was going to have repercussions. After all the months of effort I had put into the design, I had allowed one minor change to turn it into a failure. The CAD engineering team had to use their old workstations, and the perfect design document I thought I had created was wrong.

However, the next morning, I received an email from my manager.

"I have just been talking with the customer's CTO, and she has been singing your praises. She told me that your comprehensive design and performance testing allowed their operations team to quickly diagnose the 'go-live' performance issues they encountered yesterday. She said that, despite unexpected budget cuts, you adapted the design for the production implementation on short notice. She has received very positive feedback from the regional teams in Europe and India, despite some teething issues with the CAD team.

It has not been confirmed yet, but she specifically asked for you to lead the architecture design for their next ERP project. Good work and well done!"

How It Impacted My Customer

Despite some light at the end of the tunnel and some great feedback from the customer CTO, the last-minute change in the design impacted 200 end users. They had to revert back to their older 3D CAD workstations, and incurred a day of downtime during the change.

The CPU impact of using software iSCSI resulted in overall poor performance for all of the CAD desktop workloads. While not all of the server workloads were affected, the design still failed to meet one of the primary requirements, which was for performance.

In most implementations, the host CPU is never going to be designed to be at peak capacity. Though the design had headroom, estimating the peak average CPU utilization at around eighty percent, the added overhead of each host handling software iSCSI instead of the physical HBA cards was enough to degrade performance for the write-heavy CAD applications.

As a result, the customer ended up having to seek approval for 32-iSCSI HBA cards, which were needed for the vGPU-enabled rackmount hosts. Existing blade mezzanine HBA cards could be used for the application servers so the impact of the issue was limited to the CAD virtual desktops, but end-users were still impacted.

What Could I Have Done Differently?

Due to the last-minute change in the design, the impact on processor utilization with software iSCSI was overlooked. The original performance load-testing proved that the physical HBA provided excellent performance for throughput, IO, and latency, all meeting the customer's performance requirements. However, the purpose of the performance testing is redundant if the design changes at a later date. Though the budget is not directly the responsibility of the architect, it is still the responsibility of the architect to make sure the design meets the customer requirements, within budget constraints.

When I first learned of the budget constraint and removal of the HBA cards I listed this as a design constraint, but I should have called it out as a major risk. As with any major risk, the CTO should have been advised immediately, in the absence of the customer's architect, and a decision could then have been made whether to get approval for additional funds or delay the CAD engineering workloads to a later date.

What Did I Learn?

For the storage architect, Brian, software iSCSI may have never caused issues with any of his former implementations, but it is a mistake to assume that one size fits all. Just because software iSCSI is a valid option in one environment does not mean it is well suited to another. The same goes for best practices. They are simply that. A best practice is not a mandatory practice.

With the Christmas holidays fast approaching, and the design document completed, it was easy to rush the design change at the end. A design should never be rushed to completion, especially with changes that result in poor assumptions. The customer architect was my source of truth, but with him off sick, in hindsight, I should have immediately raised my concerns with the entire project team and the CTO.

Just because something has always been done a particular way does not mean it is the right way. Just like the predictable patterns of the rush to buy last minute Christmas gifts, or my daily morning coffee, we gravitate towards the way things have always been done. We are creatures of habit. Though computer systems can be predictable too, they are also complex in design and require a methodical approach to ensure a successful implementation. It is easy to overlook something, especially when considering storage as we think mostly about I/O, throughput, capacity, and latency. The demands on the CPU are not bound only by the application workloads. The role and services the kernel is performing are a factor too. In this case, the vSphere kernel had the added burden of software iSCSI in a high I/O environment.

I disregarded my own skills and expertise thinking another architect knew better. Despite having performed load-testing and getting sign-off from the CTO on meeting the performance requirements, I allowed someone else to convince me that a small change to the design would have no impact. I should have either tested that assumption or rejected the change.

I doubted my own stance on the design and took the untested advice from someone else. I was entirely to blame. We were motivated to stay within budget, but it led to failure. Had I relied on the conviction of my own experience, the go-live would not have suffered performance issues.

The Oversized Physical Exchange Server Project

This story relates to a project I was involved in as an Infrastructure Architect leading a very successful virtualization practice with a close to 100% virtualization ratio in 2015. It was mandated by the architecture board that all new applications must be virtualized. There were only a few legacy systems remaining that were either close to retirement, waiting to be P2V'd, or waiting for specific application migration projects to move them onto the virtualization platform.

The Project

One of the applications due for upgrade was Microsoft Exchange Server 2007. This company's Exchange 2007 implementation was running on physical servers, configured with cluster continuous replication for High Availability (HA). Whilst this had served the company's requirements well, the hardware was overdue for retirement and troubleshooting hardware issues had become a common occurrence for the small team that was still managing the few remaining physical servers in the datacenters.

Whilst it had been communicated to the team managing the Exchange environment that the new environment based on Microsoft Exchange Server 2013 must be virtualized due to the way internal chargeback was handled at the company (users paid per GB of storage, vCPU, and memory), it was deemed vastly more expensive to run Exchange virtualized. This was due to the high costs of maintaining the company's legacy storage arrays, as the per-GB cost of each array was determined by a separate storage team.

Virtualization and HCI

To help combat the high costs of storage another project was in progress to implement Hyperconverged Infrastructure. The new Hyperconverged Infrastructure solution would be managed wholly by the server virtualization team, lowering the costs of maintaining and managing storage.

The new Exchange 2013 platform was a great use case to run on the Hyperconverged Infrastructure due to the lower cost of storage. A business case was made to compare the operational and capital costs of running Exchange on Hyperconverged Infrastructure versus physical servers, with a clear decrease in operational (OPEX) and datacenter (CAPEX) costs by running Exchange virtualized. With approval from the architecture board, a design was started with the goal to build out a virtualized Exchange environment running on the new Hyperconverged Infrastructure platform. The Exchange team was not keen on the idea; instead, they wanted to use Microsoft's preferred architecture deployment of Exchange on physical servers to match what they were doing with Exchange 2007. Whilst this is a Microsoft best practice it did not fit the company's direction of reducing operational complexity and removing multiple architecture silos.

One of the distinct advantages of running Exchange virtualized was the reduced amount of rack space required for the solution. During the design it was decided to deploy Exchange with a 1:1 vCPU to pCPU ratio for maximum performance, with two Exchange Mailbox Servers configured per virtualization host, in a multiple cross-datacenter Database Availability Group (DAG) design. Members of the DAG would be distributed across multiple hosts, to prevent a HA event from taking down multiple members of the DAG. Because Exchange is non-NUMA[1] aware, this design allowed each mailbox server to occupy a single socket, preventing issues with NUMA cross-talk. A total of five

[1] NUMA stands for Non-uniform Memory Access, where memory access time depends on the memory location in relation to the processor. Local memory to a processor gets faster access.

hyperconverged VMware ESXi servers (for N+1) would be provisioned per site, with 8 Mailbox servers running on four ESXi servers. There would be a total of 16 Exchange Mailbox VMs deployed.

Each Hyperconverged Infrastructure ESXi host was provisioned with 256 GB of RAM, allowing each virtual machine to consume 96 GB of RAM, which was the upper limit Exchange supported as of Exchange 2013. (This is important to note for later in the story.)

The sizing was validated using Microsoft's Exchange Sizing Calculator Tool, and the design was deemed appropriate as it met performance and resiliency requirements during all failure scenarios.

Microsoft and Physical Servers

Whilst the virtualized Exchange design was ongoing, the Exchange Team continued to push their ideology of controlling the entire infrastructure stack by implementing physical servers. Microsoft even came on-board and strongly recommended that the preferred architecture on physical servers be followed for all Exchange deployments, regardless of customer requirements.

With the virtualization design finished, it was time to purchase new Hyperconverged Infrastructure servers for the deployment. To keep the Exchange Team happy, Exchange was to run in its own VMware vSphere cluster, preventing any issues with oversubscription.

Just before the servers were ordered, Microsoft threw a curveball at the design when inquiring about the storage protocol that the Hyperconverged Infrastructure ESXi servers provided. This particular vendor provided storage to ESXi using the NFS protocol, which Microsoft claimed Exchange did not support.

As every VMware Administrator knows, this claim is not valid when using ESXi as a hypervisor. This is because SCSI-based disks are presented to the guest OS with all SCSI to NFS communication protocols converted at the ESXi hypervisor, whilst fully supporting Exchange storage requirements in regard to

Forced Unit Access (FUA), write-through, and so on. In fact, Exchange is the only application that has this perceived limitation, and historically it goes back to Exchange 5.5 when it was possible to present CIFS or NFS storage directly to the guest OS and run your databases off network storage. However, Microsoft's Exchange product management team has not validated a third-party hypervisor (VMware ESXi).

Microsoft stated that because of NFS the design would not be supported and should follow the preferred architecture. The Exchange Team had won. They were going to get their beloved physical servers. The virtualization team then scrambled to implement the design on the traditional three-tier virtualization architecture backed by SAN instead of Hyperconverged Infrastructure, but again, the high costs of storage made the Total Cost of Ownership (TCO) too high.

With the project already unnecessarily delayed, the Exchange Team went ahead and ordered four physical servers per site packed with 256 GB of RAM and Dual E5-2699v3 CPUs with 18 cores each to meet the original design of the Hyperconverged Infrastructure ESXi servers, plus a bunch of Direct Attached Storage (DAS) storage filled with cheap SATA drives. Instead of scaling out the design with 96 GB of RAM and a total of 16 Exchange Mailbox VMs (8 per site), the implementation was changed to four mailbox servers per site.

At this point I disengaged as physical servers were outside my domain of responsibility. The Exchange on physical servers deployment went on without too many issues, and mailbox migration proceeded.

The Failure

After about three quarters of the company's mailboxes were migrated, issues started to arise. The mailbox servers were showing excessively high CPU utilization, which did not make sense as they were sized correctly using the Exchange Sizing Calculator (pre-version 7.5).

Users were experiencing frequent Exchange problems and the migration project was halted to troubleshoot issues. The problem was frustrating and resulted in large amounts of lost productivity as support staff were bought in around the clock to troubleshoot Exchange connectivity problems.

Microsoft support was engaged, and after escalating to Exchange engineering they had a worrying conclusion. The servers were oversized. Microsoft had published a blog article that supported this conclusion, with a new recommendation of 24 cores and 96 GB of memory as a maximum.

On the physical servers, this limitation had been exceeded as we had a total of 36 cores and 256 GB of RAM per host. Due to the size of the servers, they were trying to do so much work that Exchange was running into architectural bottlenecks and spending a lot of time dealing with locks and thread scheduling instead of handling transactions associated with the Exchange workload. So as with Exchange on NFS, the company's Exchange deployment was again not supported.

With virtualization, the company could have easily scaled out the solution and reduced the memory and CPU, as per the original design, with minimum disruption to users. When the solution was resized using the Exchange sizing calculator with 96 GB of RAM per mailbox server, it was discovered that, instead of 8 mailbox servers, 16 were required. This matched the original virtualized Exchange design. This posed a major issue as it was going to take time to both change the CPUs and memory on the existing servers, and procure an additional 8 servers with 96 GB of RAM and 24 cores.

There was a lot of finger pointing back and forth amongst various departments, but ultimately there was no choice but to purchase new servers to match the new sizing requirements. This doubled the hardware budget and datacenter costs, vastly exceeding the project budget and making the TCO of virtualized Exchange Servers significantly more attractive. Even so, as the project was halfway through the migration phase, new servers had to be purchased.

Another eight physical servers were procured, this time with 96 GB of RAM each and dual 10-core CPUs. The physical server vendor agreed to physically swap out the CPUs on the existing servers to match the new hardware, and the additional RAM was removed to reduce them to 96 GB. The DAS shelves also had to be reconfigured to distribute the drives equally among the new and old servers.

All in all, this added a lot of additional time, costs, and operational hours to the project. If the platform had been virtualized from day one, these risks would not have occurred.

How It Impacted My Customer

The following were the main impacts to the customer:

- Major widespread, intermittent Microsoft Exchange outages occurred whilst waiting for the deployment to be redesigned. This led to loss in employee productivity because email was not functioning properly.
- Huge increase in project cost and delays due to the need to purchase additional physical servers to allow the project and migration to continue.

What Could I Have Done Differently?

These are areas where I would do something differently:

- Prerequisites: After it was determined that Exchange was not supported on ESXi NFS datastores by Microsoft, this issue should have been escalated to the vendor to determine why this was a constraint. (Microsoft would have pushed back on the hypervisor as well; NFS was just the easier target.) Eventually the company would have had to decide to move forward with "limited" or "best effort" support from Microsoft, or go ahead and virtualize it.

If (when) the vendor pushed back and said ESXi absolutely could not be used, the project should have continued on virtualized three-tier servers to meet company standards and requirements instead of choosing physical servers. The internal chargeback costing issues should have been resolved earlier to provide a lower price for the Exchange Team to run their servers.

- Sizing: A major issue was that Exchange team did not perform proper due diligence on sizing their environment.
- Deployment: A more extensive test plan should have been run after the deployment was done and before mailbox migration was started to determine how Exchange would function under both increased load and during failure scenarios.
- Pushback: Poor communication was the main issue that caused this project to fail. The teams should have worked together and allowed each other to fully communicate. Too many assumptions were made on how the design should look, both virtualized and on physical servers. Proper requirements should have been gathered and documented, with a more in-depth risk analysis completed and communicated to business stakeholders!
- Shared Information: It would have been helpful to share my findings with the Exchange team, but given how that team worked; any shared information would likely have been ignored.

Something I Did Wrong

Even though I was not responsible for physical servers, as a technical lead and architect I should have offered my advice and guidance to assist the team during the sizing and deployment. Whilst I did convey the risks associated with the design running on physical servers, the risks were not properly communicated to the correct stakeholders.

What Did I Learn?

This project taught me that communication is a very important part of being an Infrastructure Architect, along with following a proper design methodology and performing risk analysis. Whilst I was aware of the advantages of Exchange being virtualized, these advantages should have been better communicated to the stakeholders. Although best practices and reference architectures are available for most products they should only be used as a reference. Customer requirements come first.

Requirements gathering and communication are key to any success, and you cannot do these without communicating and engaging the right stakeholders.

Realize What Customers Are *Not* Telling You

A few years ago, I was the front-line manager for our Systems Engineering group at the university where I worked. We had a team of committed and engaged engineers with varying degrees of skill working with VMware systems. I had recently been given an additional role as lead engineer and owned the process of modernizing the datacenter by running the project to move from the old rack-and-stack model to a flexible, virtualized environment. We were not running an actual self-service or elastic cloud, but we had saved hundreds of thousands of dollars a year through consolidation, hardware cost avoidance, and staff labor savings. We also got a new CIO.

The Project

Our new CIO was far more aggressive than any of the previous CIOs I had known over the past seven years. He did not want to talk about new projects—he wanted to see them in production. As the leader of a well-regarded team at our university, I was eager to talk to him about projects that I wanted to roll out in a pilot program on campus. The idea I was most excited about was a VMware View-based VDI environment for one or two computer labs on campus. As luck would have it, I had some time with the CIO soon after he was hired in June. I told him how bad our computer labs were at meeting the needs of our students and how the labs would often hang when academic software was run, and I proposed that we could build something that would be better, faster, and cheaper. I will never forget what he said.

> "Sounds like a game changer – can we have it ready for next year?"

In higher education, our development cycles for student-facing technology are measured in semesters. With that in mind, when our CIO said next year, I thought he meant January of next year, the second semester of the academic year.

> "Sure," I said, "we can have it ready for January. It will be tight, but we will get it done."
>
> Our CIO stared at me blankly. "No, no. Next year. September. Have it ready for when the kids come back."

I started to say something about having a POC ready in that timeframe, but the CIO was three organizational chart steps above me and I was not about to argue with him. It did not matter anyway. He cut me off and said he was looking at replacing 200 lab systems across campus over the summer, and that we would use that funding for VDI. I was stunned as he thanked me and moved on. I was suddenly responsible for the largest dollar spend I had ever been tasked with, and the deliverable was due faster than I thought it could be done!

I met with my team that day and started re-prioritizing goals and tasks. We would need to be focused to get the VDI project out the door successfully. Looking back, setting up 200 concurrent View users seems almost quaint, a simple task.... But, at the time it felt very much like the scene in the movie Apollo 13 where they dump out all the parts on the table and tell the team that they need to make a square filter fit in a round hole using nothing but the parts on the table in the next three hours, or a bunch of astronauts die.

The most important deliverable was to improve the end-user experience by delivering a much better offering to our students (who are our paying customers) than they currently had with the desktop lab systems, many of which were woefully outdated.

Being a stickler for following a process, I insisted that we walk through all of the project design stages. Our timeline was super tight but we would not just wing it and hope everything turned out well. We started by collecting requirements. We met with faculty who taught in the computer labs, spoke with academic administrators to understand what they cared about, and spent hours with students asking them what they used the computer labs for. We got a clear picture of what we wanted to build: an always-on, readily available VDI environment that would have great performance for SPSS (statistical analysis software), MATLAB, and other academic applications.

Knowing what we wanted to build, we benchmarked what students already had. We timed everything from power-on, login time, and application launch time, to running a controlled process in multiple applications, and got averages back for each lab. We even had a professor develop a statistical model to put our proposed environment through its paces. We gathered a lot of data about what students currently had.

We had concerns about how some of the applications would perform over PCoIP, but none of the academic applications had any full-screen high-delta video or animations, so we became much less concerned. Our use case was just about perfect given the limitations of our network and 2013 VDI technology.

We built the new environment with the goal of optimizing our most important metric, average academic application performance, and we were successful. We reduced application load times by over 70%, reduced calculation times in apps by an average of 50%, and software failures or crashes were reduced by 90% or better. We were excited to bring it to our test groups.

We invited faculty to join us while we had students use the system as we observed their usage. Students walked through multiple real-world homework problems or projects as we observed load and performance on the host servers. Everything seemed to be going well, and in a roundtable discussion afterwards, we got uniformly rave reviews. It was much faster and it was “cleaner” than they were used to. We were thrilled to be ready for production buildout.

By then, it was late June, which was perfect because our budget cycle is July through June and funds become available at the beginning of the new fiscal year. We purchased production hardware as soon as the books opened and built fully ready new lab environments in record time, ahead of schedule. We performed a final production load test on August 15th and were ready for students on August 16th. Terminals were installed the following week, and by the time students were moving into the residence halls we were congratulating ourselves on a job well done.

I was especially proud of how we had involved the customers. Students and faculty were involved the entire time and we took great care to solicit and adapt to their insight and feedback. I was presenting the project as "customer-led" within IT and to the campus executives.

The first week of university classes is an "all-hands-on-deck" event for IT workers. PTO is not granted and it is expected that everyone will be ready to handle any and all incoming requests. Usually, my team did not handle front-line support tickets, but during that first week I turned over the entire team to the Help Desk as auxiliary support for any VDI-related tickets. I cleared my calendar so that I could be anywhere needed during those first few crucial days.

The Failure

On the first day of classes, I got up extra early (I could not sleep anyway), went to the gym for my morning cardio, and headed to campus. I wanted to see students use the new vLabs (our internal brand for our VDI environment) terminals in the library. I do not know what I expected to see, but I guess I thought students would be dancing between the bookshelves and crying with joy over the new terminals or something like that....

When I got to the library, it was just after 7 a.m., which meant that there were no college students around. (I do not know about you, but when I was in college, "morning" started at about 10:45 a.m.) I wandered around to see if anyone was in a different wing of the lab and not finding anyone, I sat down in a chair, brought out my laptop, and tried to bounce some email out of my inbox.

From my position I could see the entire room. I will never forget the first student I saw use vLabs "in the wild." This student came into the library about a half hour after I got there and walked over to the open access terminals. He must have immediately known something was different, because he looked at the tiny Wyse P25 terminal, tilted his head to one side, and walked to a different table. After he realized that all of the computers had been replaced he sat down at a terminal.

Again, I did not know what to expect. It was the first day of classes, and classes had not yet started, so there was no way this student had homework to work on. Perhaps, I thought, he would log on and recreationally fire up an equation editor or something. That did not happen....

The student logged on, and I started ticking off the seconds until it got to a functional desktop. He reached into his backpack, and I anticipated him pulling out a textbook to get to work. Instead, headphones came out. I thought that was curious, but maybe he wanted to relax and listen to some music as he worked on his calculus, right? He turned back to the desktop and it was ready to go. I watched, smugly thinking how much better than last year his experience already was. I wanted to hang up a "Mission Accomplished" banner. He poked at the P25 terminal for a bit and after finding the headphone jack, plugged in his headphones and fired up Chrome.

No worries, I thought. Chrome works perfectly in our environment. I thought he was going to download some work in progress, but no. He fired up YouTube, searched for something, and hit play. After the obligatory advertisement faded, a music video popped up, which he promptly put into full-screen mode and it played back horribly. I doubt that this video was running at 10 frames per second. It was not cinema-quality for sure. It was more like an 1800's flipbook.

In less than 15 seconds, the student yanked out the headphones, loudly declared "this piece of [expletive redacted] is some bull [same expletive redacted]," jammed the headphones back into his pack, and left the library!

I sat there, completely speechless, and thought something must be wrong. I walked up to the same terminal (which he had left logged in, not caring about security) and plugged in my ear buds. I went to a different video site thinking perhaps YouTube was broken, but I had the same bad video experience. Video, especially full screen video, was trash!

Within hours, we had multiple student complaints that the computers were slow or that they seemed broken. It was only a few days before student sentiment was that VDI was a huge step backward over the run-down, dumpster-candidate desktops they used to have. Not good for half a million bucks, right?!

We spent the next few weeks desperately trying to figure out how to make our VDI solution, which was optimal for computational homework, be even moderately acceptable at video. We had missed something really important. We had failed to capture an unspoken student requirement. The solution had to be good at watching videos and wasting time, not just cranking through homework.

Ultimately, an almost complete redesign was required. It took my lead engineer and me several days to figure out why video was so bad. Simply put, the PCoIP process was consuming virtually all of the available vCPU when it was required to compress and ship 1080p video down to the terminal. It was not designed to handle that case. We had under-provisioned compute.

How It Impacted the University

The University got negative feedback from students for deploying a solution that they hated. On our campus, like many others, student technology is funded from a fee paid directly by students in their bill. So, these students paid every semester for these labs, and they were upset that the labs did not meet their expectations.

I spoke to Student Government and promised that we would get it fixed, which we eventually did. Though you can make a case that production use was not impacted, a large percentage of commuter students spend the day on campus but do not have a dorm room to go back to, so they spend time in the libraries or student union with their friends. In a very real sense, video access made their days more bearable.

This experience demoralized my team and shook our confidence. We thought we had a great solution and were excited to have built something we thought would improve the student lab experience. Instead, we ended up looking like jerks.

What Could I Have Done Differently?

First and foremost, requirements were not properly gathered. We asked students what they used the computer labs for. Any student knows the response to that question is to explain how studiously they work on assignments, and nothing else. Except, that is not true. Never has been.

I should have had people (possibly student employees) sit in the labs before we modified anything and report back on what applications they saw in use. Video would have come up very quickly because when you walk through the labs you see people watching YouTube, Netflix, or other video on many screens. It is ubiquitous.

An alternative would have been to get student feedback by asking more open-ended questions in an anonymous survey about what they think is important. The challenge with a survey is that you generally get poor response, so if I did it again, I would give the students an in-person anonymous feedback form immediately before and after their initial tests.

The biggest failing was not getting students, our primary customer, in front of the technology in an unsupervised environment and getting ad hoc feedback afterward. In other words, we failed the UAT (User Acceptance Testing) because we collected the wrong feedback. We did not get the whole picture. We had compressed the UAT phase aggressively to meet our deadline and did not execute it properly. If we had deployed several terminals and let them be used in a natural way we could have identified this gap in expectations and delivery. If we had identified the problem sooner we would have had time to correct it. We needed only modest additional hardware to make it work better, so we could have prevented the problem.

Finally, we should have kept faculty and student feedback sessions separate. Professors are focused on making sure class delivery and academic work are successful, but are less concerned with the school/life balance that our students care about. By having two sets of stakeholders in the room with differing views, the group with more power or seniority will overshadow the other group. Students are conditioned from grade school to defer to teachers, so having professors with them in the room was a mistake.

What Did I Learn?

I learned that not all requirements are voluntarily given to you by your users. Sometimes they do not tell you something that they care about for a variety of reasons. In hindsight, in this case it seemed like there was an unwillingness or embarrassment to admit that they were using the computers for more than their academic workload.

However, I think users frequently have assumed requirements that they do not communicate because they think they are so basic that they do not need to describe them. For example, if you asked someone what their ideal car is, you might hear about it being electrically powered, or having leather seats, or an awesome infotainment setup. However, very rarely would someone say it needs four wheels because that is an assumed requirement. Users do not feel like they need to mention it because it is so basic. The issue with assumed requirements is that they are assumed, and you and your users may have a very different understanding of the use case.

I also learned a lot about different stakeholders articulating different needs. For example, if you were building a finance application, the accountants might detail needs related to pivot tables, click-through analysis, and the ability to reconcile multiple accounts, but they do not say anything about wanting to generate purchase orders quickly because they do not do that. However, if you talk to the buyers in the company they only talk about generating purchase orders. We tried to combine all stakeholders as one user group, and it was a miss.

Ultimately, we ended up having a very successful VDI deployment because we paused, listened to our users, and did not "dig in" and hold to an untenable position when they had negative feedback. We accepted that we missed an important requirement and we figured out how to fix it. This was not a fun experience, but our customer satisfaction at the end of the academic year was fantastic and set the stage for years of success.

The Workload and Requirements Matter

As a partner consultant, I completed most of my projects the correct way. But...to be honest, there were projects that only happened because a vendor or salesperson offered a customer a great deal on some new gear, and we were brought in to perform an upgrade, replacement, or integration using the new gear.

There is nothing quite like trying to build a decent implementation plan after the deal has been sold, when the new gear is already onsite, and the clock is ticking. If you have been involved in such projects, whether as customer or partner, you understand that there is little time to perform all of the usual design work.

The Project

This story begins with a deal that was sold by someone else. This deal was led by a storage array vendor and my team was engaged to perform data migration services. It was a new storage array, the latest model, and the goal was to replace two old arrays that the customer was currently using.

The intent was good: get the customer's workloads onto the latest technology, with faster cache and disk access times, a streamlined management toolset, a less expensive warranty, savings on licensing, and get them prepared to protect their data by replicating it to a DR (disaster recovery) site. The cost to keep a legacy array under support and maintenance is very expensive when you get outside the normal window. The customer's savings from licensing one array instead of two at the production site, and reducing the payment for support, would free up funds to help fund the new array for their new DR site. So, everyone's heart was in the right place at a high level.

To make the decision even easier for the customer, they wanted to upgrade to the latest version of their virtualization platform, but the old arrays were no longer supported as of this new version.

The shiny new array was one of the first units off the assembly line. My team had not seen this new model, but we were told that it was just an upgrade to the models we had been deploying and supporting for many years. When it arrived, the vendor installed it, and we proceeded with a typical data migration plan. Most of the storage on the existing arrays was for virtual machines or backing for file shares. We were able to easily relocate virtual machine workloads using capabilities of the virtualization platform (we all love Storage vMotion, right?). File shares were migrated using proven methods with minimal downtime as they were synchronized, and a reboot was performed during the outage window for the final swap. All of it was standard, and it went smoothly.

Performance of the new array was noticeably better than the old ones and the migration proceeded faster than planned. We finished the migration and ran through the usual post-migration checks to make sure the data was consistent on the new arrays. In the morning, the business owners validated that they could see their data and virtual machines. The old arrays were decommissioned by the storage vendor and removed from the customer's site over the next couple of weeks.

The Failure

A few days after the arrays were decommissioned and removed, we received a call that performance of the new system was terrible, users were complaining, and virtual machines were dropping off the network.

Uh-oh.

As a partner, I wanted to help my customer, especially as I was familiar with the virtualization platform they were using. By the time I was called, the customer had already placed calls to the storage vendor, their network vendor, and the virtualization platform provider. They had started collection of logs from all over the environment and had tried rebooting some hosts and virtual machines. Nothing seemed to help, and rebooting a virtual machine actually made things worse as it struggled to even boot the operating system.

We looked at everything we could think of. We saw high latency on the datastores, but nothing to explain why. Then, like magic, everything was fine. Huh?

Everything remained fine for nearly a week while we continued to monitor and collect logs on a constant basis. Without a repeat performance of our issue or an identified trigger, the teams chalked the problem up to an anomaly...shaking the bugs out of a new system.

Then, it happened again. Not on the same day or at the same time as before, but the same behavior.

Okay, that is bad. Everyone was questioning, "What is happening in the environment right now?" According to the customer, there was nothing out of the ordinary, just business as usual. No month-end processing, no special promotions or events, nothing that would put additional load on the system. Just a typical day; just like yesterday when everything was working fine.

So, more calls were made, more logs were sent to all support teams involved, and everything was escalated. Without anything concrete to look at, we were hip deep in a "spray and pray" situation. We managed to exclude the IP network from the issue because the storage array was connected via Fibre Channel, and connectivity between networks seemed fine even during the outage. We had made some progress, but we still had no answers. At least we had captured detailed logs when the issue happened this time and, hopefully, had caught something at some level in the technology stack.

Being curious and wanting to help in any way that I could, I set out to dig through a massive collection of logs. My team was only involved with changing out the array, so I figured that was the logical place to start. At least, it let me focus on a subset of the pile of data we had collected. Unless there was an incompatibility between the array and something else in the environment, there had to be something going on in the array itself. At least, that is what I thought. Heck, it was a new model, and those never have issues, right?

I quickly discovered that simply organizing the logs was a challenge, never mind understanding everything that I had, and chopping them into manageable pieces. Gigabytes of log files would not load into most text editors in Windows.

Meanwhile, the problem cropped up at random times, not predictable intervals. The customer was not happy as everything had been working well before the array replacement. I was unlucky enough to be present during several heated, closed-door meetings with the director of IT and customer executives. There was talk of ripping out the new array and putting the old ones back in service or, worse, going with another storage vendor. Putting the arrays back into service would be a challenge as they had likely gone to that big datacenter in the sky a week earlier.

The threat of changing to another vendor encouraged the current storage vendor to engage their über technicians (the guys who live in the steam tunnels and read hexadecimal) to check out the array. We had the big guns. The array and the entire storage network had been given a clean bill of health down to the firmware levels on the host bus adapters (HBAs), but since they were coming in cold, these guys wanted to start from scratch and revalidate everything. They found no known incompatibilities among the current components in the environment. That review had also been performed during the pre-sales assessment, and was accurate. Too bad! A simple explanation would have been welcome....

I had other customers and projects, but I worked long into the evenings and early mornings trying to find anything that would explain what we were seeing. I do not like not knowing why something is broken, so it became a bit of an obsession. I had narrowed the window down to about an hour, but there were many attached systems and many data points spread across many logs. I had a tool to help visualize the data contained in some of the logs, which helped a bit, but did not provide a holistic view and only operated on one log at a time.

At about 11 p.m. one night, I saw something that looked wrong. Mind you, I do not spend my days reading log files or traces from storage arrays, so it took me some time to think through what I was seeing and to make sure the time frame was correct. Plus, I was tired and did not fully trust my ability to reason through the problem at the required level.

What I saw was the dominant workload personality changed nearly immediately from read-heavy to write-heavy. Not just heavy: there was pretty much a 100% about-face on what the array was being asked to do at a time just before the issue was reported. I still have nightmares about that graph. I checked with some other parameter values at the same time of this inflection, easier to do once you had an exact time to look for, and the data seemed consistent. Something in the workload changed.

If you are familiar with storage, you know that spinning disks are slow, so they put RAM (cache) in front of them to compensate for the slowness. For the read cache, there are a variety of predictive algorithms that watch for access patterns and try to make informed decisions about what data a user may require next. These algorithms can preload the read cache with the data that the user may need and provide a great experience when it guesses correctly. In a large storage array, there are typically a lot of disks and correspondingly, more cache. Usually, the larger cache means the data that a user requires has a better chance of being there when requested, so performance is great. (I have vastly oversimplified this, and I apologize to storage people out there, but I wanted to review the high points for those without a storage background.)

There is another side to caching: the write cache. Different vendors implement caching in different ways, but the general concept is that a write is committed to the cache, and a response is sent to the user. A commitment is required so that the system requesting the write knows that the data has been written somewhere. Committing to cache is much faster than waiting for the commitment to disk, so performance is improved. Furthermore, if the same data is requested for reading, it is pulled out of this cache, so the immediate re-read is really fast too. At some point, the cached data is written (committed or de-staged) to the spinning disk for persistence. Unless you are living dangerously, your write cache has a battery to keep it online in the event of a power outage, so there is some level of persistence in the cache, although I would not call it permanence.

Cache is not infinite. So a situation may occur in a busy array in which the write cache is full, and the data cannot be accepted to the cache. At this point, the write cache is bypassed, and the data must be written directly to disk. In this case, performance is reduced because the workloads must wait for acknowledgement of their writes to (slow) spinning disk that is currently so busy that the cache is full…so, extra slow.

This was worse!

In this particular array, the read and write cache were shared in a ratio based on the majority profile of the work being requested. What I was seeing was a complete switch from mostly read to mostly write, which meant that the amount of read cache was greatly diminished to make way for the increased need for write cache. When you think about it the logic is sound: I am writing more, so give me more fast space to handle the incoming writes. However, this meant that the other workloads were effectively starved out because their reads had to go to disk without the benefit of cache. And the disks were busy trying to handle a massive increase in writes, which are actually more "expensive" than reads.

So…what gives?

As it turned out, the application development group periodically dropped their database and reloaded it with a very large (terabytes) known dataset so they could run validation testing of new application builds. Their test machines were large Unix systems in a cluster configuration, built just like their production counterparts. When they did this, which could be at any time, the majority workload on the storage array became writes, the personality of the cache switched to compensate, and performance of everything on the array suffered.

Before the arrays were replaced, the second array in this customer's environment was where the development team's testbed was hosted, and it was basically the only workload run there. The problem was introduced by collapsing the two-array solution down to a single array. Even with a faster array, the diametrically opposing workload types created a pathological contention situation. To add to the excitement, this job took several hours to run, so a developer would kick off this job right before leaving for lunch or going home for the day. So, nobody was around who knew that this workload had been added to the array's load or could help us correlate the issue to the cause.

This story does not have a happy ending. The storage array vendor we were working with had another type of array that would allow partitioning of the cache and offered further mechanisms to isolate workloads that could not play in the same sandbox. Sadly, though, the customer had lost confidence and was not interested. They engaged another storage vendor to come in to move them to that vendor's higher-tier array, which also had the partitioning feature. On the plus side, I hear the customer is doing fine—they are still in business over a decade later.

How It Impacted My Customer

There was quite a bit of pain experienced on a frequent basis as this issue was triaged and the root cause was identified. Unfortunately, because the storage array was a global service that hosted all virtual machines in the customer's environment nearly all workloads and services were impacted. The performance impact was so significant that everything was considered down when the issue manifested. This downtime translated to poor experiences for the customers of our customer as well and likely loss of revenue and confidence in the customer.

Ultimately, it resulted in a negative rating for the storage vendor and, to some extent, my company, which had only been brought in to migrate data between the arrays, but was part of the implementation.

What Could I Have Done Differently?

The following areas could have approached differently:

- Requirements: Though I was not part of the sales process and I was working on a deadline, a more thorough identification of requirements beyond, "customer requires X TB capacity, which can be provided by this new array, which is faster than the current ones" would have been good. The requirements gathering process did not include real data to support workload modelling for resources.
- Workload Segmentation: Contention and security issues caused by overlapping workloads must be well understood before proceeding. Development and test workloads were running on the same array as production workloads, without any segregation. There should have been defined guidelines on acceptable use cases for deployment to the production environment.
- Pushing back: In this case, the requirements gathering process was cut short in an effort to get the deal done so that the customer could realize the cost savings. The value of gathering data in an environment to support requirements cannot be overstated and it would have been smart to push back in the face of vague requirements. They may have just found someone else to perform the work, which, in the end, would have been less stress for me.
- Appreciation for uniqueness in the environment: The implemented design was based on a cookie-cutter model that was likely developed according to the 80/20 rule, but it did not necessarily fit this customer's specific use case. Especially as this customer was consolidating from two arrays down to one, which, in my experience, was unusual at the time.

- Test cases: This relates to the above requirements issue but warrants specifically being called out here. It would have been good to have test cases to address all of the workload profiles in the environment, not just the normal ones, but due to the scale of some environments, it is not often possible to test *all* of the workload/application profiles. We usually rely on data metrics, use cases, and representative workloads. Testing *all* applications can add months of time and a higher cost. This is why we work with customers to consider use cases and representative workloads.
- Architecture: Like workloads, hardware solutions have different personalities and fill different needs. It is critical to understand the benefits and limitations of any piece of gear. Despite the sales incentives and marketing messaging, no tool is right for every job.
- Run away: While running away might have been a relief, it really was not an option. However, if you are in a situation where you have had a flaming bag of bad decisions dropped on your doorstep.... Nah, I guess running away is never the right response. But, being involved earlier in the process to prevent those bad decisions would have been good.

What Did I Learn?

Despite a pervasive notion that one size fits all, due to dramatically different needs and personalities, certain combinations of workloads can create a contentious environment when sharing the same resources.

There is no substitute for collecting data to drive requirements. Without understanding the current state, the success of any sort of migration will be a roll of the dice: you may escape unscathed or you may lose it all.

Untangling issues by searching through tens or hundreds of gigabytes of log files takes a lot of time even if you know what you are doing and what you are looking for. Most systems at the time could not open files that big, much less search through them. The `grep` utility is your friend if you have an idea of what you are looking for. The needle in a haystack is a real thing, and some of those pieces of hay look an awful lot like needles until you chase them through the stack and get them isolated.

Persistence and cooperation are key to troubleshooting complex issues in shared environments. Though I found a weird-looking period of workload inflection in one of the log files, it was not the whole answer. It took working with people who had very in-depth understanding of how these things behaved to reach an explanation. Remember that you do not have to be the smartest person in the room to provide value. Everyone can contribute, even if it is just by coming at a problem from a different perspective. Working with people who know more than you do is a great way to learn!

Design for the Right People

A couple of years ago, I was brought on as the lead architect and implementer to help design and build a Cloud Management Platform (CMP) for a very large, worldwide manufacturing company. I had done this many times before so this seemed quite ordinary at the time. This customer was a "problem child" as they had difficulties laying out precise requirements, suffered internal strife and disorganization at the management layers, and engineers engaged in power plays attempting to usurp authority to glorify their own positions.

The account team brought much of this to my attention, but I had heard almost all of it before. "No matter," I said. "I will coax everything I need out of them during my design session." And so, POs were signed, calls held, introductions given, and project management assigned. I scheduled a trip to visit the customer site and conduct the in-person design session. In these sessions, I customarily follow a pre-defined method.

1. Gather all stakeholders in the room including business sponsors.
2. Introduce the technology.
3. Explain what they can expect from an infrastructure perspective.
4. Introduce the prerequisites literature that they were responsible for completing.
5. Begin to document their provisioning process as it exists today.
6. Gather requirements for the process as it may change.
7. Note any constraints in their environment.
8. Work on achieving a design of the end product, keeping the previous steps in mind.

Of course, there can be some variations. But, generally, the idea in these sessions is to build a work plan so that I, as the architect and implementer, know what to build, how to build it, and what functions it must ultimately achieve.

The Failure

During the day-long design session many people came and went, from managers to executives, and finally the engineers. One individual stood out because of his constant outspokenness and, frankly, rudeness. This individual, who I shall call Bill, was the manager of a separate application team and a peer to the manager acting as primary stakeholder and customer project liaison. Bill demanded the CMP must look a certain way, have exactly a certain functionality, allow exactly these users access, and provide exactly those catalog items for customer deployment. Needless to say, Bill was quite a handful, and he bashed the CMP product at every opportunity as its limitations were explained.

The primary stakeholder and customer liaison, Jim, was also present, and I constantly looked to him to ascertain his comfort level with Bill's marching orders. Jim offered very little pushback and his protestations were quickly squelched after Bill made it perfectly clear that his group of users were of paramount importance. It was, in effect, a bespoke CMP for Bill, with my marching orders coming directly from a Major, despite the General being in command.

After some back-and-forth with Jim to confirm, in private, that Bill was allowed to drive the project, Jim seemed to be OK with proceeding. "Yes, sir," I was inclined to say, having been given the green light to design the solution and begin building.

Fast forward a couple of weeks and the CMP was built, the catalog was available, and things were working well. "Excellent," Bill said, "this is perfect." I gave myself a hearty pat on the back and was met with a series of congratulatory calls from my account team. I was told "They have never said anything from us was 'perfect' before!" I thought it was a job well done. The only remaining piece was to conduct a showcase demo session with senior customer executives to show off this shiny new, costly CMP that had taken a couple of months to build. I was a little nervous because things had not gone smoothly, mainly due to Bill's impertinence and the often confusing directives he gave me.

Demo time. I had practiced all catalog items beforehand. I made sure the system was blazing fast, in perfect working order, and fully branded with the customer's logos and color schemes. I had rehearsed multiple times how I would progress through the system, and I could find no flaws. The remote meeting software began to chime in my ear as people joined the meeting. It seemed half of the executive leadership was on this call, far more than the invites I had sent out, and more than our account team had indicated would attend. I was calm but soon could feel the first bead of sweat break out across my brow. Never mind. Keep going. I walked through the catalog, deploying item after item, showing request forms, buttons, and drop-downs—everything that I had gone to great lengths to custom design. And it was significant. The pages looked like an online order page from Hell, but everything worked and was "perfect" as I kept reminding myself, Bill's words of triumph still echoing in my mind.

The demo was all a blur in time, but it went swimmingly. Nothing acted up, no catalog items failed to provision. Yet, there was total silence. Five seconds elapsed. Ten.... I had to speak; the silence was killing me.

> "Can I answer any questions or perhaps show a couple other catalog items I built for you, if you have time?" I asked. The response came quickly and sharply.
>
> "Why in the Hell is there so much crap in this catalog? And why on God's green earth are the forms asking for so many inputs from our users?! This is way too complex for them. Who told you to do this?!"

In that moment, I think I lost temporary consciousness, but I am not sure.

How It Impacted the Customer

Although not a typical failure situation in the sense of a catastrophic service outage, this particular scenario still had profound consequences for availability at the customer and decreased confidence in the partner.

This CMP was supposed to be the centerpiece of the customer's IT environment and represented a huge shift in mentality and operational process from laborious, manual, email-driven requests to consolidated, push-button, sleek IT-as-a-Service with full governance and auditability. After all of the delays in getting equipment, setting up meetings, and agreeing on terms, the customer had a very tight deadline to roll out this service. And because of mistakes during implementation, they had missed their deadline. The CMP had to be pushed back even further, costing additional millions of dollars because the support contracts for the legacy systems used to keep this untenable process afloat had to be renewed.

Management, all the way up to the CEO, was furious. Bill, who had been so outspoken before, was as quiet as a specter and was nowhere to be found. IT teams suffered, and confidence in us as their partner of choice was lost despite our doing everything per instructions. I could not believe this was happening!

What Could I Have Done Differently?

I had to ask myself, was this even my fault? After all, I was told it was perfect by the guy calling the shots. How did we go from perfect to train wreck? It was as if a grenade had been lobbed into our bunker. I have never felt like such a failure after being virtually assured of success.

Although he was certainly the most vocal, Bill really was not the most important person on the project. This CMP had many other stakeholders, some with even more to gain (and lose) than Bill and his team. I had no idea. Where had they been? It came down to, as IT often does, people and process and lack of communication with other parts of the organization. I should have anticipated this and pushed back, and engaged our account team and practice manager to make sure we were engaged with all of the stakeholders and an appropriate level of higher customer management. The correct people should have been found, and they should have been brought to the table. And during the design process, those people should have seen a preview and provided sign-off so we did not find ourselves in this sorry state after so much time was invested. The entire project needed much more visibility in the customer organization to flush out the people who would ultimately depend on it.

What Did I Learn?

Lack of communication can kill you.

Technology is, ultimately, a people problem, no matter where in the project continuum you find yourself. Do the best you can to find the true lines of business, stakeholders (there will be many), and any sponsors on the customer side before you start your design. Shop that list around with everyone on it to see who might be missing. You can easily get into a “too many cooks” situation, but validate that list of sponsors and stakeholders high enough up so you cannot be blamed for not bringing them to the table.

The loudest voice should not always get the most attention. Sometimes, a customer group may have a limited view that could benefit from important holistic commentary from your support crew, such as the account manager, project manager, and others outside of the architects and engineers working on design and deployment. Everyone has an opinion, but some opinions are more important than others. An opinion may be less valuable if it is out of context, or if it is a personal opinion without scientific or technical evidence.

Finally, as a rule of thumb, status calls should be held regularly with key stakeholders to facilitate understanding and alignment of project progress and decision points.

If You Want to Win You Must Lose

As I thought about what story to tell I wondered what single story encompasses all of the most valuable lessons I have learned. I could not come up with a single story, so I decided to tell two stories that together covered many of the most valuable lessons I have learned. In this story, and in the following story "You Own It All," I have distilled down my failures for review and, hopefully, this will help you to avoid my mistakes. Failure, though unpleasant, can be very instructive.

The Project

This was not the first time I had implemented a Virtual Desktop Environment (VDI) environment, but it was early in my career. I worked for a credit card processor and was tasked with building a PCI-compliant VDI environment. Little did I know at the time that PCI[2] has nothing to do with security and everything to do with compliance, but I was about to learn.

I designed the environment to use VMware View as the VDI front end that would run on Cisco UCS[3] with a Tintri storage array on the back end. I was told that we needed a secure way for our contractors to access sensitive information. It was a perfect use case for VDI, and I began building soon after a short requirement gathering session. One of the major issues I discovered was that the company had no 10Gb/s switches—there were only 1Gb/s connections in the datacenter. This was a problem because NFS over 1Gb/s was not a supported configuration. I needed to find a way to use the storage we had, without spending any more money. The solution I came up with was to connect the Tintri array directly to the Cisco UCS Fabric Interconnects (FI), which were all 10Gb/s.

[2] In this case, PCI stands for *Payment Card Industry*.

[3] Cisco UCS is the Cisco Unified Computing System, a datacenter server computer containing computing hardware, virtualization support, a switching fabric, and managed software.

The Failure

I thought I had solved the issue, but in fact I had introduced a single point of failure, and I was going to be the one to trip over it. This configuration worked only while the primary Cisco UCS FI was up and running. If the UCS FI had to fail over, the virtual IP address on the Tintri array had to be manually moved to the secondary connection so it would communicate on the secondary UCS FI. I explained this risk to the company and documented the process for maintenance.

Meanwhile, I made a classic engineering mistake and just started building. I thought all of the requirements had been gathered and all of the issues solved, so I built out the connection brokers, security servers, and so on. When done, I reviewed the system with the stakeholder. And while reviewing, I discovered that due to other constraints the entire VDI environment had to be in one flat IP space! I spent the next week undoing everything I had built and re-doing it to accommodate the new constraint.

At this point I imagine you are screaming that building a VDI environment in a flat IP space is a bad idea, and I agree. However, this was the requirement, and I built it as they requested.

A few weeks went by and the Horizon environment was humming right along with happy production users. Friday, mid-day, I went down to our datacenter to do some work in one of the racks. Being a credit card processor meant datacenter access was an ordeal. We had security guards, several layers of sealed doors, and cameras everywhere, so it took a while to get in.

As I was working in the rack that day, I needed to pull a few cables out of the secondary Cisco UCS Fabric Interconnect. I grabbed the cables and pulled them out of what I thought was the secondary Cisco UCS FI. At that moment my phone rang,

"Good Afternoon, sir" I said to my boss on the other end.

"The VDI environment is down. Can you jump in and look at what is going on?"

"Sure can, I will get right on it."

As I hung up, I looked in my hand and wondered if the set of fiber uplinks I just unplugged could have anything to do with the problem. I had picked the wrong Cisco UCS FI and when I pulled the cables, I caused the Cisco UCS FI to failover. When the failover occurred, I lost the storage to the VDI environment.

How It Impacted My Customer

VDI went down and desktop users were unable to work. This lasted several days, costing the company tens of thousands of Euros in lost productivity.

What I Could Have Done Differently?

First, I should have verified that I was pulling the right cables.

Even more important, I should have gathered all of the requirements before designing and building the environment. I should have taken the time to fully document and design the environment before I started building. It is very tempting to just start building and get the work done, but that can cause issues that impact the project. You may end up re-doing work, and not delivering value to your customer.

I should have asked why the gear was not labelled on the racks.

During the tag in and tag out procedure, I should have checked if the locator LEDs on the UCS FIs were used.

Finally, I should have asked if it had been verified, using the UCS control panel, that the expected FI was in the lead.

What Did I Learn?

I began to learn to push back, a lesson I continued to learn more about in the coming years. People make mistakes all the time, but we build in redundancy to make sure that the systems we build stay available for as long as possible. By not pushing back, I had introduced a single point of failure that I would later, ironically, trip over. Even if I had not pulled the wrong cable, something would have eventually exposed the issue I had created, and it really would have been my fault.

Final Thoughts

You may be wondering why I titled this story “If You Want to Win, You Must Lose”. Within this title is one of the most important lessons I can pass on, and this lesson is reinforced in the story “You Own It All.” You can learn more by losing or failing than you do by succeeding or wining.

You Own It All

This story encompasses many lessons that I take with me into every new project.

Have you ever seen a war movie where soldiers are walking though enemy territory and one of them steps on a landmine and hears a little click right before the explosion? Though a bit dramatic, I think each of us has experienced that moment where we wish we could take a few steps back....

The Project

A few years ago, I was brought into a manufacturing client's project to help them set up a disaster recovery (DR) failover environment for SAP. If you have never run or deployed SAP, just know that it is a complex beast. SAP is a suite of applications that all interconnect and roll up into a single application. I am not an SAP or database expert, so our company brought in two other consulting firms to assist on these areas of the project.

- One firm dealt with the complex tasks involved in taking several SQL clusters that were using Windows Failover Clustering and converting them to SQL Always On.
- The other firm provided SAP experts. They dealt with the setup of SAP HANA, the in-memory SAP database, and enabled it to failover into a secondary node.

The entire DR environment was designed and implemented in Microsoft Azure.

On the first day of the project a lesson I learned long ago came back to me. Inside most projects you will find "landmines." Pre-sales engineers try to identify the landmines, but until you get into the details onsite you do not know what you do not know. The pre-sales people likely identified some landmines and had some idea of where others were, but when you are on site it is your job to find them all. (I have become better at finding landmines before I step on them and hear the click, but I have stepped on my fair share...)

As we spent the day deep diving into SAP, SQL, and HANA, I learned that this project was going to be more difficult than I had thought. The plan itself was straightforward. Convert the SQL clusters to SQL Always On, and put one of the three nodes for each cluster in Azure so that if the primary site failed the database would be recoverable and ready to go. A similar tactic would be used for SAP HANA: set up a new SAP HANA node in Azure, set up data replication, and in the event the primary site went down, fail over to the SAP HANA node in Azure. SAP HANA requires some manual intervention, but a runbook would be written for that. As for the SAP application nodes, DR software would be used to replicate and protect the nodes to an Azure region. If the primary site failed, the client would log into the console and recover SAP application nodes into Azure.

The plan was straightforward enough that it might have worked. We finally finished our day of deep dives into the massive application diagrams that show how SAP functions and how the different SAP servers make up all the sub-applications. I explained that Azure does not support shared disks. This was one of the reasons that SQL was being refactored to a SQL Always On cluster in which no shared disks are required. Everyone was on-board with that plan.

The Failure

There were multiple failures on this project.

SAP Applications on SQL Servers

Before wrapping up for the day, I asked for a list of the application servers with a breakdown of which parts of SAP they ran. As I read over the list, I saw something strange. The server names looked oddly familiar. I realized that they had given me the names of the SQL servers, not the application servers. A simple mistake, so I asked again if I could see the application servers. The person I was working with said, “you have them,” and then I heard it…that little click as I stepped on the first landmine. "Are you telling me that you loaded the applications on the SQL clusters that are hosting the databases?"

Long story short, yes, they had loaded the SAP applications on the SQL servers, and furthermore, they used Microsoft Clustering to fail over the application server. Because of this, I could not replicate the SQL servers or application servers into Azure. The only solution was to rebuild the application servers into standalone VMs that could be replicated and protected with Azure. This was the right answer, but it was out of scope for the project. We spent the next week convincing the client that this was the only path forward. I had to explain the strategy to the president of IT and get his buy in before we could move on.

Limited Maintenance Downtime

We finally had our go-forward strategy. Rebuild SQL clusters and migrate the databases, build a second SAP HANA server in Azure, and after the business rebuilt the application servers, replicate those into Azure as well. Seemed easy enough...what could go wrong? Turned out that the business used SAP to operate 24x7, so the only approved downtime was the third Sunday of every month. This meant that the business had to build and migrate application servers, and stack cutovers, until the third Sunday when they were deployed. Deployment took months to complete because of the limited maintenance downtime and pushed us past our estimated time and hours for the project.

Load Balancers

During this time the firm running the SQL migrations was hard at work doing their builds, migrations, and cutovers. This generally went well, but was not without problems. I was not closely involved in this part of the project, but even if you do not own a part of a project you should track the details as much as possible. This is not because the people doing the migrations had issues, but in hindsight, if I had paid closer attention I might have learned something about the SAP environment that could have helped later.

Weeks passed and the work continued. Application servers became standalone VMs and I added them to the replication plan with no issues. The first application server was tested and booted in Azure. I saw what I thought was light at the end of the tunnel.... We talked through plans for testing the larger parts of the SAP application and scheduled those tests. I developed the DR runbook, and spent several long meetings reviewing and double-checking all parts of it.

During the final review session all I needed was final signoff on the DR runbook. After going through the runbook, I asked if anyone had any questions. Someone asked,

> "After we failover how are the users going to access the environment?"
>
> "Well," I said, "We will update DNS to point to the new public IP addresses and they will access it as they always do."
>
> "Great", the person said, "and I assume then that all the sub-domains will change as well?"
>
> "Sub-domains—what do you mean?" I asked.
>
> "Well yeah, the load balancers read the domain information and direct the request to specific ports on application servers."

There it was again, the all too familiar click of a landmine....

Keep in mind that we were months into this project, and there had been many deep dives on current architecture. This was the final review of the DR runbook, and load balancers were mentioned for the first time! I realized at this point that a deeper dive into the SQL server migrations and application server rebuilds might have revealed the hidden load balancers. I am not sure, but when they reviewed the connection methods for the sub-applications, I might have noticed the load balancers that no one had mentioned. Fast forward a few weeks and another pushed deadline, and I had the load balancers set up and ready.

Big Bang Full SAP DR Test

The plan for the DR test was to take and test single application stacks one at a time to flush out any issues, fix the issues, and execute a big bang full SAP DR test. The system was extremely complex and the information I had gotten thus far was not entirely accurate. This approach would enable us to catch issues and remediate them before we were committed with the business watching. We were in the weekly meeting leading up to our first major single application test when we were told that the business could not afford the time it would take to test all of the systems separately. It was too close to the end of the fiscal year, and the project needed to close. Despite pushing back, I could not win this battle. We were out of time because of the application server rebuilds and missed load balancers, and we had to proceed with the big bang full SAP DR test.

The day before the big bang full SAP DR test we met for our final go/no-go decision and ran through the pre-checks. During this review I noticed that all of the servers, which had been replicating perfectly for months, were now about two hours out of date. After some troubleshooting, we discovered that the software used to keep the VMs protected with Azure had stopped replicating, and we could not find the reason why. We opened a P1 support ticket and were promptly told to check all of the things we had already checked. We said that we had done that, and heard nothing back for days.... While waiting for support, we discovered that we could still failover VMs into Azure, but they were 24 hours old at the time of the test. This was not a major issue as all the real data was stored in the SQL databases anyway.

The morning of the test, we failed over application servers and they came up as expected, but they were stale as replication for the last 24 hours was missing. Then, we encountered the first of many issues that we would have discovered if we done the micro DR tests as originally planned. The first set of servers was up and running, but the client could not log into them. We later discovered that this was because the time was off by 3+ hours as the application servers were on the West coast and were failing into the East coast.

Then, we ran into Kerberos issues. The local admin passwords were rotated every 24 hours by their security software. Because these images were more than 24 hours old, the password vault no longer contained the correct password for the local admin password. Along with these issues, after about 20 VMs had been failed over we started getting recovery error messages due to an IO cap within the Azure storage account the disk images were in. Overall, the application tests went very poorly and we did not hit the mark. However, the SAP HANA and SQL tests went well, and data was written in Azure and successfully transmitted back to the production site.

Success?

After a Hellish weekend of fighting to get a successful DR test, and having heard nothing back from support, the replication of the SAP application servers miraculously "fixed itself" on Monday at 2:30 a.m. To my utter amazement the client called the DR test a success! When I asked how that was possible the client said that, because the data portion went well, they were confident that they could get SAP up and running following an actual DR event. According to the client we had discovered the issues they would need to remediate to get the SAP application servers up and running.

How It Impacted My Customer

This project was an utter failure even though the client called it a success. It did not impact production or do anything that the business deemed a failure, but I view this as substandard work because we never completed a full DR test. This failure could impact the client in the future if there is an event and they need to use the DR environment. One could argue that if the client is happy everything is good, but in this case I would disagree. There are times when we must push our clients as much as possible to a better standard.

What Could I Have Done Differently?

There were many points at which I could have done things differently and changed the course of the project.

- I should have gotten deeper into the application server rebuilds, and the SQL server rebuilds and migrations, with the client.
- In hindsight, when I discovered the applications were installed on the SQL clusters, I should have requested that we deploy an application mapping tool. This would have given me more data on the SAP environment. They were changing the environment drastically as they were building new application servers. I should have known the design documentation we had was not accurate anymore, and the output from a tool like Azure Migrate would have been helpful.
- I should have insisted on a micro DR test before proceeding with the big bang full DR approach. We would have discovered the time issue and almost all of the other issues we encountered during our actual DR test.

What Did I Learn?

We did a lot of remote work during this project, and people commonly multitasked during our meetings. I should have required people to be more focused and engaged. I learned that I can insist that people focus and pay attention, without having to nag people, by setting vision for the project.

I was the lead architect, and even though it was not my job to do the work, I learned that I need to take more ownership and provide some oversight. I would have been able to catch some of the landmines we stepped on had I been more involved. Thus, the title of this story, "You Own it All." As the architect, I am responsible for *all* parts of a project. This does not mean that I must be the expert or own all the pieces, but I need to understand what is going on in all areas of the project.

Final Thoughts

We can all learn from each other if we are humble enough to acknowledge and share our failures, and listen when others speak. It is impossible to know everything, and technology moves so quickly that even if you did know it all, you do not know it all now. Take advantage of our lessons learned—you do not always have to learn the hard way. Look at my tracks, and walk away from that charred bit of land where I once heard a click.

The Underground Fire

Cities are constantly evolving and growing over generations. And just like a tree, there are layers and histories to the rings of evolution and growth. Sometimes growth spurts have consequences that are not seen for years until the right set of circumstances occur. This is the case with a small power connector that failed and ended up causing an explosion, and an underground fire that took out communications and datacenter infrastructure affecting much of the coast.

The main players in the story included:

- ITAR power, an electric company that provides service to the state.
- BigCity Center, a skyscraper in the central business district of downtown BigCity that provides datacenter real estate to multiple datacenter companies.

Within BigCity Center is an MMR (Meet-Me-Room). This is a place within a carrier hotel where telecommunications companies can physically connect to one another and exchange data without incurring local loop fees. Services provided across connections in the MMR are voice circuits, data circuits, and Internet protocol traffic.

This disaster occurred in 2008 but is still relevant. In 2008 cloud was not as pervasive as it is today. AWS had been launched only two years earlier and Microsoft Azure and Google GCP did not exist. Datacenter and colocation facilities were the only way to provide infrastructure to companies that required high availability and high bandwidth. This was a requirement for many organizations to function.

If you had a business in BigCity that required IT infrastructure and you did not have your own dedicated facilities, chances are that you either had some equipment in BigCity Center, or you were using services from a service provider that had equipment there. To use cloud terminology, you can consider this to be an *availability zone* within a region.

A cascading series of events occurred that effectively shut down all operations at BigCity Center for several days. This outage affected thousands of companies and prompted many organizations to re-evaluate their business continuity and disaster recovery (BC/DR) strategies in the years to come.

The Failure

It was a nice sunny weekend, which was rare for this rainy coastal city. I was riding into work on the train, coffee in hand, shaking off the fog of the weekend. I had some work to do in the datacenter, but not until later in the day. In the meantime, I hopped into a coffee shop and proceeded to find a comfy corner that I could sit for a few hours while I downed a second cup of coffee. I heard some sirens down the street but did not think much of it as sirens are not uncommon in any city. More fire trucks were coming, and that could not be good, especially given that all the buildings around were concrete and constructed with built-in anti-fire measures. If one or two trucks came, maybe it is a fire drill, but this many? Something had to be wrong. I packed up my things and decided to investigate. There was smoke coming from somewhere, and you could smell it. The fire hoses were plugged into fire hydrants and ran down the streets, and the area was blocked off so no traffic could pass. Word-of-mouth reports indicated that there was a fire in a manhole and flames were shooting out.

In BigCity, because of the population density in the city core and rapid expansion of business in the latter half of the 20th century, the power grid was put underground in a dual radial underground system. This was managed through about 800 manholes with 146 circuits coming from three substations. According to the post-incident analysis report, the root cause of the fire and subsequent explosion was as follows:

> The root cause of the failure of circuit C12357G20 was due to an overheating connector on the 600A load break elbows of the Y splice on one of the phases. This probably occurred over a period of several hours, which caused the melting and thermal decomposition of the polymer components of the Y splice and the accumulation of combustible gases.
>
> The fire was initiated by the power arc on the overheating connectors of the Y splice on circuit C12357G20 which caused the polymer components to catch on fire resulting in further decomposition of the material and accumulation of combustible gases.

The fire was two blocks away from the BigCity Center and knocked out power to about 2000 customers in the area. The datacenters were also affected, but they switched to generators, which had more than enough fuel for days of operation. No-one was impacted at this point other than customers without backup power.

A vast amount of water was required to combat the fire. This was taking water pressure away from some of the other buildings in the area, including BigCity Center. This failure model had not been accounted for in the design of BigCity Center, and the generators that supplied power to the building were designed to be cooled by water. The generators started to overheat because they could not be sufficiently cooled due to the lack in water pressure.

It was around this time that I got a call from a coworker.

> "They want us to shut everything down!"
>
> And I said, "We cannot do that! The DR site is not ready to take on the entire load and we have never tried a fail-over yet!"

We were working against time with no idea how much we had left.

If we tried to do a planned fail-over, we needed to let all of our clients know what we are doing and when.

If we ran out of time and power during the failover, that might cause more problems such as data corruption or some services with dependencies failing to come online. This might make the recovery process and total impact to our clients even greater.

If we did not follow the planned failover process and instead forced an immediate failover we could save some time, but the risks were just as great. Clients would be in the dark and service-level agreements (SLAs) would be broken. Powering down all servers gracefully and keeping them offline until the power was back up and stable would have the least impact to the infrastructure, but it would be disastrous for the relationship with clients.

We did not know how long the outage would last. That would be determined by the fire department, ITAR Power, and the BigCity Center facilities department, and they were not collaborating real-time....

To address the problem we did a combination of the following:

- We categorized services as critical and non-critical. In this case, critical was communications-oriented only. This included phone systems (IP-PBX) and email systems. All application servers, file services, databases, VDI, and so on, were deemed non-critical. It is not that they were less important, but we could not risk their corruption using a failover plan that was not validated, and we did not know how much time we had left.

- A communication to customers explained the issue:

  Emergency outage due to fire; affecting primary and secondary power systems. Communications systems including IP-PBX and email will be failed over to DR site immediately. All other systems will be unavailable until the incident is resolved. Please log off all systems as they will be preemptively shutdown in 15 minutes. Some congestion may be experienced on the IP-PBX system due to the increased load on the DR environment. Incident updates will be provided every two hours via email and in real-time on our service status page.

We broadcast this communication to keep clients in the loop, and started to shut down VMs, hosts, backup systems, and lastly storage systems (that we could). The IP-PBX systems were the easiest because the systems were already in-place and clients were already able to use them. The main difference was that we had dedicated hardware at the primary site that could accommodate up to 1000 concurrent calls, whereas at the DR site we could only do 200 calls in software. Not ideal, but better to have a degraded service with some availability than no service.

During the process of failing over our email systems, we got worse news. The HVAC systems had shut down and the temperature in the datacenter was rising! Without proper cooling, the servers were going to overheat, damaging the CPUs, memory, motherboards and the hard drives. We were left with two choices: abort the failover and gracefully shut down the email servers, or try to keep the servers running long enough to complete the failover. We opted for the second option. We made sure that all other devices that are not critical to the failover process were shut down, and I made a call to a friend.

> "I need some meat curtains, duct tape, and box fans right away. No time to explain..."

With those materials, we jury-rigged ducting to help with the airflow. We looked at our watches and the server chassis temperature stats. The HVAC normally kept the datacenter at about 22 degrees Celsius (72 degrees F) and the servers would normally be at around 40-50 Celsius (104-122 degrees F), but the fans were not keeping up. The temperature was rising; 50, 60, 70, 80, 85. It finally stopped rising at 85 degrees Celsius (185 degrees F), but we knew things would start failing at this temperature. The failover process completed and we shut down the remaining hosts and storage. We had critical services up, but we were limping along and other issues arose.

- The phone systems were plagued with one-way audio on some calls. This was determined to be because of a transcoding issue on some of the systems.
- Incoming emails were fine, but outgoing emails were bouncing. This was due to a dirty IP address space that was distrusted before we purchased it.

After the fire department extinguished the fire, they still had to wait for the temperature and air quality in the underground to clear enough for the ITAR Power team to go down and assess the situation. Power was diverted from another path, and water pressure was restored, allowing the generators to operate as intended.

The incident was over, but the post-incident review continued for quite some time. It was determined that there was no way to have prevented this incident without substantial investment in modifying the core infrastructure architecture. BigCity has a higher density of power circuits running underground than many other cities. Also of note is that many utilities, including ITAR Power, used to use asbestos fire-resistant tape on the wires to prevent the sort of runaway fire that occurred. However, they removed the tape and stopped the practice due to health concerns. No replacement for the tape has been implemented yet.

How It Impacted My Customers

This incident forced clients to use manual processes and queue up work, on-premises where possible. Many clients were unable to conduct day-to-day operations for up to 48 hours because of lack of access to application servers, VDI, and file services.

What Could I Have Done Differently?

There were several things I could have done differently.

- Conduct more testing on the DR site for all services.
- Review capacity calculations per site and make sure that sufficient resources and performance capabilities are available.
- Schedule periodic DR failover and failback tests.
- Run both sites as active with the capability to automatically fail over with sufficient remaining capacity.
- Run a metro-cluster across two availability zones (datacenters).
- Improve DR runbook operational workflows.
- Work with clients to make sure that client-defined critical services are spread across multiple availability zones, or regions, with a business continuity strategy.

What Did I Learn?

- Never assume that a plan will work until you test it. Having a DR process is not the same as conducting a test of it on a regular basis and improving it every time with a gap analysis.
- Expect everything to fail, and then try to find a reason why it will not fail. This will help save you from a false sense of security. Fail-proof your design!

- Understand what is important, and prioritize services based on user feedback. What you think is important, may not be the same as what your clients think is important. In this incident, some clients were completely unable to conduct business, so the services that were up did not offer any benefit to their situation.
- Open communication is paramount. Because we were completely transparent with our clients about the situation and provided constant updates and communication, because we were all "in this together," we did not lose any clients.

A Watershed Moment

Many different kinds of disaster can affect a datacenter, but this disaster had an unusual beginning. A few months prior to what became known as "the event" we had installed a secondary cooling system to provide redundancy for the existing system. This worked well, and based on previous experiences with cooling system outages, we were confident that we had in place the necessary cooling with regards to cooling capacity, and redundancy in case of a failure.

As everyone knows, some kind of failure is always on the horizon. It is just a matter of spotting the potential failures, and doing the best you can to reduce the risks. Sadly, none of us had anticipated the pending failure, partly because our due diligence had not been good enough, but also partly because what happened was beyond our imagination.

The Failure

It was the middle of winter, with snow covering the rooftops of the building where the datacenter was located. The datacenter was placed one level below ground level, with another level of offices located below it. There were also offices located above the datacenter. All in all, we thought that good datacenter placement in the middle of the building would be reasonable insurance against flooding. We were wrong!

The Flood

On the day of the event, the sun was shining, and snow covered the ground and roof of the building. It was cold, but not freezing. The IT Operations team was happy as there were no big issues and it was business as usual. Suddenly, we got alerts that the main file server was no longer responding. The phones lit up with employees calling to report trouble and it was clear that something was very amiss.

I ran up a flight of stairs to the datacenter, opened the door, and stepped in. I will never forget the sound of my shoes hitting water as it splashed around my feet! The entire floor of the datacenter was covered in water. I could not understand how the datacenter got flooded. There were no water pipes in the ceilings, floors, or walls, and it was a secluded room without windows. It was located below ground level, but not on the lowest level of the building.

Luckily, the water had risen only to just above the wheels on the racks and had not flooded the uninterruptible power supplies located at the bottom of the racks, which would have been catastrophic. The file server that had dropped off the network moments earlier was one of the last servers that had not yet been virtualized. The IT Operations team had repeatedly postponed virtualization because this server contained so much data. As a result, it was still running on a standalone tower server and was not placed in any of the racks.

Upon visual inspection, I found the source of the water. When the secondary cooling system had been installed, holes had been drilled in the outer wall to connect to the outside module of the HVAC system. The holes had not been sealed after the pipes had been brought through. Snow was melting on the roof and accumulating in a flower bed outside of the building. The flower bed was frozen so the snow built up against the wall.

When the sun came out, the snow melted. Water always finds the path of least resistance, which in this case was through the holes in the wall and into the datacenter. The solitary tower server was placed against the wall were the holes were and all of the water that was on the floor had run *through* the server while it was powered on! No wonder it failed and dropped from the network. No one knows how long that trickle of water flowed through the server but I think it ran quite a while before failing.

Fortunately, there were a couple of small holes in the floor of the datacenter where cabling had previously run. These holes acted as drains that kept the water from rising above the rack wheels and inundating the many Uninterruptable Power Supply (UPS) systems installed in the racks. Directly below the datacenter there was a tiled bathroom, so we guided the water down those small holes in the floor to drain most of it. Some of the team dried the floor and shoveled away the outside snow that had not yet melted. The rest of the team went about restoring the system.

The File Server

All in all, we thought, we only lost that one physical server and it should be fairly easy to recover. We would create a new file server VM, restore all the files from our tape backups into it, and we would be good to go. It might take a while, but all other systems were still running. Our users could still use all of the other applications, and if they had to cope without some home directories and file shares for a while, they could manage.

We quickly created a new VM, installed the backup software agent into it, and started a full restore. It ran for a couple of hours, and then we got a new call from a user who was wondering when the Customer Relationship Management (CRM) system would be available again. CRM system?! The CRM system was not affected by the file server outage; it was running as it should, and we had no indications that there were any issues with it. Then, we realized that the Oracle drivers that the clients relied on for connectivity to the CRM system were located on a file share that was no longer available. To make driver upgrades easy for IT Operations we had placed them on a mapped file share and every client in the network used that share for those drivers.

Since we had just started a file restore and were waiting for it to complete we had no idea when the drivers would be available again. There was no way for us to prioritize restores after we had started a full restore, and ultimately, we had only one option: abort the restore that was in progress and start a new one to only restore the folder that had the drivers. Our users recognized the stress we were under and patiently waited for hours to get access again. Unfortunately, they were idle while waiting. After we got the drivers restored and fixed our mappings the CRM system was again available to everyone.

We continued to do bite-sized restores over the next week, avoiding huge restores that would take a long time. We went through the backups, looked at the folders, prioritized them into a matrix, and performed restores based on priority.

It took over a week to restore all of the files and make them available to the users again. This was due to a combination of factors including the backup software used, backup methodology, and slow tape libraries.

How It Impacted My Customer

A physical site mishap caused a file server failure, which in turn made other systems unavailable even though the other physical systems were not directly affected by the physical file server failure. The business "flew blind" for quite some time while the IT Operations team had no idea that users could not access the CRM system.

IT Operations had for years failed in their push for funding of a secondary off-site datacenter. Funding was provided quickly after this incident, along with snide remarks from the CEO asking if we had done this on purpose to get the funding. Nothing could be further from the truth. None of us wanted to work around the clock for a week just to prove a point!

What I Could Have Done Differently?

The file server should have been virtualized a long time before the event happened. This would not have prevented the flooding, but a virtualized file server would probably have been easier to recover.

Utilizing a single file server created a single point of failure that should have been avoided. If we had used Microsoft Distributed File System (DFS) or something similar we could have eliminated this single point of failure. The original plan was to configure DFS and migrate to several virtualized file servers utilizing it, but as is often the case, this kept getting pushed back in the priority queue.

The end result would have been the same if the file server had failed for other reasons, but it is interesting that this outage started with a simple water leak.

What Did I Learn?

IT Operations needs to be aware of risks to their physical datacenters and make sure that adequate risk-aversion measures are taken to prevent single points of failure. If you identify a risk in your operations, remedy it quickly! Do not postpone implementing a solution or think you will get to it later. Later never happens, and everything that is temporary is permanent until it is not.

Do yourself, your employer, and your customers a huge favor by completing work to reduce risk. Document the risk, and if you need funding make sure those who make budget decisions understand the risks involved if no action is taken. If a problem happens, and it inevitably will, it is important to have documented the risk beforehand.

It is not enough to categorize system priority based on importance. While a matrix of business-critical systems and their priorities is crucial, it is not complete unless all supporting systems are included in the same matrix. In this case, the CRM system was deemed critical for the business, but no-one had taken into account that we had a single point of failure for access to it; namely, a file share on a non-clustered file server.

Though our backup regime produced good backup tapes, tapes were not optimal for restores. Do not underestimate the time it takes to restore millions of files from a tape library, where the backup software spreads the files over all tapes in the array. In this case, there was only a few terabytes of data to restore, but the sheer number of files and slow access and seek time of the tape device caused long delays. Testing the recovery plan in advance would have identified how long the recovery process would take.

Stuff Happens and Recovery Matters

I led a team assisting a hospital (the customer) with datacenter modernization and consolidation work at their BigCity1 site when a major new release of the hypervisor came out. The new release arrived with great anticipation and fanfare, and a decision was made to upgrade directly to the new version at our BigCity2 site, and then go back and upgrade the BigCity1 site.

The Failure

While I proceeded with the BigCity2 site roll-out, I left a colleague in charge of the BigCity1 site upgrade. After a couple of weeks things were proceeding as planned at the BigCity2 site. The BigCity1 site was ready to be upgraded and my colleague conveyed the procedure to one of the customer's technicians.

They successfully completed one part of the BigCity1 upgrade together, but it was late and my colleague decided that it would be best to complete the upgrade the next day. However, the customer's technician wanted to put what he had learned into practice, so they agreed that he would continue alone with the second part of the upgrade.

The next morning on my way to work I received a distress call from my project manager, asking where I was and what I was doing. I was only a few minutes away from the site, and early, but we stayed connected until I saw him pacing back and forth in front of the customer CIO's office.

Upon straightening my collar, which was about all the time I had to do, we entered, and the CIO told us in an abrupt manner to have a seat.

> "Gentlemen, I want to know why one of my hospitals is unable to access part of its services this morning. I want to know when it will be fixed, and I want to know how this happened."

It was the first I heard of this, but I committed to both finding the root cause and restoring services as quickly as possible. The next hour was spent raising every alarm we could across the entire infrastructure stack. We got everyone in a room or on a call only to, unfortunately, point fingers at each other. Or, at least, that is what most participants were doing. A lone technician from the hypervisor's vendor and I got on a separate bridge, got a remote session going, and began to examine the issue. The technician chimed-in only a few minutes later.

> "That is weird. I see that the hypervisor is installed but, when I go to where the VMs should be, all I see are the operating system files."

Some of you may have experienced a similar situation, so you may know where this is going. A brief discussion followed.

> "You are not using boot to/from SAN, are you?"
>
> "No."

Early hypervisors did not have a lot of logic around host bus adapter (HBA) detection. During an upgrade, if you were not paying close attention while repeatedly clicking Next, or if you did not first unplug the HBAs, you were likely to overwrite one or more of your datastore logical unit numbers (LUNs) with a fresh install of the hypervisor.

Having discovered the issue, we focused on restoring the virtual machines we had overwritten. Unfortunately, this was before the development of hypervisor-friendly or integrated recovery solutions. The backup solution the customer was using claimed to have a bare-metal recovery capability, but when tested it did not work with VMs. At least, not VMs that did not already have an OS on them (which kind of defeats the definition of bare metal…). No OS? Oh well.

The customer had not had many positive recovery experiences with their backup solution, despite it being one of the best-known solutions in the industry. Luckily, most of the virtual machines at this site were the product of a physical to virtual migration effort, so we decided to try and locate the physical servers, re-migrate them, and use that as a base for our recovery efforts. Many of the servers had already been decommissioned, with drives removed and tagged for destruction, but most drives were still waiting to be collected or had not yet been destroyed or recycled.

After collecting material, reassembling servers, and organizing the order drives were in so that disk arrays were valid to boot from, we put our plan into motion. After reviewing with the customer which services and workloads were highest priority, we restored those first and, over the course of a very long weekend, we got everything back up and running.

The customer was happy with how we handled the situation and recovered their applications. We made up lost ground in the project timeline, continued with our datacenter modernization and consolidation efforts, and ended the project on a very positive note.

Despite the problems and complications, the customer continued to use that inadequate backup and recovery solution for years after the incident; not because they were happy with it, but because they had already invested so much in the solution.

How It Impacted My Customer

Hospitals operate 24/7/365. Thankfully none of the unavailable systems were patient-critical or life-supporting, but any loss of access to patient-related systems can cause a cascade of issues that impact patient care. And inaccessible systems coupled with the loss of data create opportunities for mistakes and error, and possible exposure to lawsuits. Thankfully for all involved none of that occurred.

What Could I Have Done Differently?

I should have kept to the original plan and pushed back. The events that occurred could have happened at any time, but deviating from the original plan created a direct opportunity for them to occur. If we had kept to the plan and come back after finishing the original scope of our work to perform the upgrade, these issues might have been avoided.

Be vigilant and provide oversight. Though it can be difficult to learn to trust others, it is necessary in a large project or program. You cannot be in all places at once and you have to accept that people will do things their own way. Giving your team the freedom to make decisions on their own is critical for a successful mission, and equally important to the teamwork and human elements of our jobs and careers. It is also critically important to develop a plan, keep to it when possible, make sure standards are agreed-upon by everyone involved, and be vigilant and accessible. Provide course correction as appropriate.

If I had known my colleague was leaving the customer technician alone to practice on a production system, I would have asked him to stay and provide oversight, or asked the technician to wait until the next morning. Production systems are not appropriate environments for unsupervised practice by inexperienced personnel.

What Did I Learn?

The lessons I learned are interrelated.

- Keep to the plan but be flexible. Some adjustments can be made, but discuss them with and get agreement from stakeholders. Adjust the scope of work if required.
- Be accommodating but cautious. Focus on the project scope of work.
- Take ownership. A team leader must lead the team and ensure alignment on the project.
- Test your recovery solutions often enough to be sure of a satisfactory result, because you never know when stuff can happen.

Every Step Counts...

I wrote about this particular project to emphasize the significance of every single milestone in the lifecycle of an architecture assignment.

The Project

Once in a while, a transformational project comes along that is meant to change the way an organization runs its IT group and does business. This opportunity was initiated as a series of RFPs (Requests for Proposal) aimed at the digital evolution of a healthcare provider that focused on breakthrough research and treatment of critical care patients. There were multiple phases in the vendor process, with Phase 1 involving the network and communication, while Phase 2 covered server, storage, virtualization, and Virtual Desktop Infrastructure (VDI).

I was working for a Global Systems Integrator (GSI) at that time, and we were one of the key contenders for the project. I was involved in Phase 2 as the lead architect for the delivery phase. We had been awarded the Phase 1 contract, and Phase 2 was almost certainly going to be awarded to us as the customer wanted to have a single implementation partner. As expected, we submitted the RFP response and after a couple of presentations, won the project. This was a massive win for our company.

Such critical RFPs and projects tend to come with extremely strict timelines and that was the case with this project. The timelines were strict, the testing criteria were even more stringent, and missed deadlines were associated with financial penalties.

After we got over the excitement of winning the Phase 2 contract, we kicked off the architecture phase for the server/storage part of the project. First, we checked the BOM (Bill of Materials) as we had a broad range of vendor involvement including Cisco, IBM, VMware, Citrix, and a number of application vendors.

We were working on an architecture involving two sites with 80+ blades and rack mount servers, using VMware vSphere 5.5 as the virtualization layer, and Citrix XenDesktop infrastructure to cater for 1000+ concurrent VDI users. We also had to consider the associated application gateways and load balancing appliances.

We started by architecting the Cisco Unified Computing System (UCS) servers for the implementation of the VMware virtualization layer, which would eventually host the corporate servers as well as the Citrix XenDesktop environment. The storage design was taken up simultaneously to make sure we had all of the requirements captured. We went ahead with an integrated approach, looking at all of the moving parts in the project.

We revisited all of the requirements provided to us in the RFP, as well as the items discussed during the design workshop. The idea was to make sure that the design incorporated all of the correct specifications for the servers allocated to the various environments, with correct storage sizes assigned. Some of the items included in the design were correct disk group configuration and LUN specifications, with the respective SAN and zoning specifications for the SAN. We kept predictability and consistency in mind while configuring the MAC, WWNN, and WWPN pools in the Cisco UCS, and maintained this across the sites. We worked on the architecture keeping in mind the overall requirements of oversubscription, availability, and manageability. The same requirements would be used to integrate the various components in our phase of the project and then, eventually, connect to the main network.

The next step was the design of the hypervisor environment. Some of the questions included:

- How many servers per cluster?
- Will virtual switch configuration be VMware Standard Switch (vSS) or VMware Distributed Switch (vDS)?

- How many uplinks are required from each host?
- What about the datastore configuration for the respective environments?
- What about the availability configurations?

Project Details

We have discussed different high-level aspects of the architecture, so now we can dive into the details. The server environment comprised of blade servers for the corporate clusters, with the blade chassis connected to FIs (Fabric Interconnects) with an oversubscription ratio of 4:1. The End-User Computing (EUC) environment was meant to have rack mount servers, and these also connected to the FIs, to provide a single connection point between the main network and the Datacenter Compute. The blade servers as well as the rack mounts were dual-homed to the FIs, which were then dual-connected to the datacenter leaf switches.

Five VMware ESXi clusters were included as part of the design to host production servers, along with VDI, DMZ, Unified Communications, and management workloads. The same cluster configuration was to be available at both sites, which were designed in an Active/Standby mode. The customer was a Cisco networking shop and wanted to maintain a familiar configuration experience on the virtual networking front, so the Nexus 1000v was positioned for the virtualization environment. Another purpose was to provide centralized network configuration and management.

Storage was IBM, and standard configuration, carving our LUNs for the respective clusters and workloads. Cisco Multilayer Director Switch (MDS) was included in the design for the SAN and there would be asynchronous replication. There was a requirement to use FCIP (Fibre Channel over IP) for inter-SAN replication between the sites.

With these relatively standard requirements, the design was finalized and presented to the customer for review while parallel discussions were initiated with procurement teams at the customer's and our end to start working on the order and lead times for delivery.

The Failure

Then we were met with a surprise! The customer told us,

> "Here is the thing team, while you were working on the design, the equipment was ordered and is already on site."
>
> Our response was, "But we just submitted the low-level design, and the understanding was that the equipment would be ordered soon after."

The customer and service provider had worked together without the design team's knowledge.

Remember, we discussed the strict timelines that come with these transformational projects? Well, dealing with the change in equipment (before design was complete) was the first of a number of things we would do "in the interest of time" to meet the strict project timelines. So we took this as an opportunity to start building the base configuration and get the foundations laid for the environment while the customer reviewed the design.

Did I miss anything in the overall architecture description so far? Oh yes, network configuration! What about the routing and the switching and our requirements for inter-site replication?

The network project was awarded and their design phase had started earlier than ours. Did we order the Phase 2 equipment along with the network? Well, not really. The network equipment was delivered a while back, and the team is halfway through the configuration. We were supposed to have detailed design meetings after submitting the initial draft to work on integration of the two project phases as a number of our requirements are dependent on the network. But I thought, it is not too late, we can still do it. We are one team and can deal with it internally.

We got into the detailed design discussions and learned that the network was a spine and leaf architecture, and the ToR (Top of Rack) switches would serve as the connectivity point to the server environment. We worked as a team and got things on track.

There were a couple of minor issues, but we overcame them and were finding opportunities from the challenges posed to us. But, we hoped the surprises would stop so we could actually work towards a successful implementation.

We started to move forward from there. We knew we had a good project plan, we knew our deployment milestones, and we had already done the base work. The ordering process was brought in line with our timelines and also had the correct discounts and alignment with the sales cycle. That should allow us to get right into the hands-on work we cared about.

By his time, the low-level design had been provisionally approved for both the network and storage tracks, and we got a green light to proceed with the customer-specific steps in the implementation cycle. The first step was validation of the delivered equipment. We checked the hardware, then the cables, and then the software images and licenses for all the software.

Things were progressing well. We were able to build the server environment at the primary datacenter and interconnect everything as per the design, and even the storage integration was completed on time. We installed VMware ESXi on the servers as well. Great work so far! We were on-track to deliver the project on time. Maybe the early ordering was a great idea?

As expected, the management cluster was the first one to build, but before that, we installed the vCenter server. Another easy step.... The server was installed and we got to the point where we had to install the license on the vCenter server.

Where were the licenses for the hypervisor environment? The project manager had them, so we waited for his email containing licensing information, and we started the license fulfillment process. After we had the host licenses we asked for the vCenter license and the response was,

"What vCenter license?"

"The vCenter license that was part of the BOM (Bill of Materials)."

"Well, we ordered what was in the BOM."

We checked the BOM, and the vCenter license had been missed. We decided to order the license ASAP and persist with the evaluation mode until we got it.

We hoped that everything else would be in place and that this was just another small problem. The compute and storage environment were ready to integrate with the Core Data Center Network. We knew we would be connecting across to the datacenter leaf switches using a non-blocking configuration while dual-homing the infrastructure. Easy…right?

Yes, it is a very easy step. Just connect the cables according to the connectivity map, and it should be good to go. But that only works if you have the required optics (small form-factor pluggable transceivers [SFPs]) to achieve the connectivity. The optics were not ordered by the Phase 1 team because they did not know how many were required, and the Phase 2 team did not order them because we thought the network team would take care of it.

You get the developing trend, right? Missed items were causing delays. We noticed a number of other items missing, some of them related to storage replication licenses, incorrect line cards on the storage switches, and so on. This was not the first such project we were doing, so what had happened here? We took a step back and started a due diligence process. We revisited the ordering steps, and reviewed the delivered equipment to see what we had and what we had missed. We noticed more missed items. Some were more critical than others, but they were all going to cause project delays.

Lost time, hits on the overall project bottom-line, and of course lost effort. At this point we had to accept the situation and take the project to completion. From then on, we were careful to avoid any unforeseen issues and make it a seamless deployment for any future project.

This project was eventually delivered successfully but there were some delays to the timelines. We were able to avoid penalties, but the loss of our team's credibility and self-confidence were the biggest cost. We went back and analyzed the project as a team, and took a lot of lessons from this experience to avoid similar issues in future engagements.

How It Impacted My Customer

The major impact to the customer was lost time and project budget. The mistakes were, by and large, on our end. Items were missed in the BOM, steps were skipped in the process, and there was a lack of coordination. The timelines for the customer were affected. We worked to minimize the lost time, but the project delivery was still completed late. Testing was delayed, and other vendors involved in the project were affected by the delay. Because this was a hospital, the cutover and migration of systems and patients could only be done with advance notice, so schedules needed to be rearranged.

How It Impacted My Team

The impact to my team was much broader. People, process, and profitability of the project were all affected. People were held at the project for longer than intended, and this affected the overall project costs. The process was changed for various reasons and the normal order of operation was not followed. Still, the biggest pain point of all was the lost credibility with our customer, which we recovered by putting in extra effort and adding resources to minimize the time impact.

What Could We Have Done Differently?

We should have worked as one team. Even though the submission was in two separate phases, we should have had a single team work on it with representation from all stakeholder teams. An enterprise IT infrastructure is comprised of network, compute, storage and virtualization, and none of them can operate without the other. Therefore, all of the architects for various tracks need to contribute to the final design.

Follow the process, and give equal importance to every step in the process. The pre-sales cycle is as important as the sales cycle, and all are as critical as the delivery itself.

Follow all steps in the correct order. If you do things differently for any reason perform due diligence before proceeding with the change. The impact needs to be assessed for every change.

What Did I Learn?

When I wrote this story, I reflected on all the work I have done with enterprises and it was a wonderful trip down memory lane. As I remembered projects, initiatives, and architecture opportunities I have taken on, I also recalled instances where the design was incorrectly done, something was missed during implementation, requirements were not properly analyzed, or other issues caused unintended results. To keep a project on track keep the following in mind:

- The first step is as important as every following step. Follow the project plan and treat all steps with equal importance.
- Update the project plan after every change and perform a thorough impact analysis of every change.

My story is for an on-premise greenfield deployment, but it applies to all variations, whether an on-premise deployment or a cloud implementation, or a step during the hybrid cloud journey. Every step is important, and the project and all planning and design documents are living documents until the project is completed. Remember, any change in the process can and will affect all others.

The Longest Work Weekend

I was the company's virtualization administrator and maintained the VMware infrastructure on a day-to-day basis. I planned and executed a VMware vSphere upgrade from 5.5 to 6.0 for an environment that was not very large, but it hosted the main virtual infrastructure and all critical applications of the business.

The second phase of this upgrade left me with broken and corrupted Platform Services Controller (PSC) replication partners and a corrupted database, requiring me to work long weekend hours with support.

The Project

Change management at this company was so stressful that it made you feel paranoid about everything, even causing you to doubt your own technical abilities. The change management process was very stringent. If the requested maintenance window was not met, the consequences were dire — upper management often shouted at people! I do not miss those Change Advisory Board (CAB) meetings!

The environment consisted of four sites running VMware vCenter Server 5.5 on Windows with embedded SSO (Single Sign On), all in Linked Mode between four major US cities. VMware Site Recovery Manager (SRM) was configured with protection groups between all four of the sites in a kind of mesh topology. This added some complexity, nothing too crazy, but it was an additional dependency to consider.

The vCenter Server upgrade alone comprised of two phases, not counting upgrades for hosts and VMs that were scheduled for a later date. The paranoia about changes at this organization forced people to be very methodical which, of course, is not bad. Unfortunately, only a few changes could be incorporated at one time, even if they did not directly correlate to each other and would not cause any issue. The CAB did not like to see multiple tasks involving different systems scheduled for the same maintenance period, even if they could be done at different times within the timeframe.

The first phase of the project, which had been completed successfully weeks earlier, deployed four new Windows servers to be used as external vCenter SSO servers, one at each of the four locations. Then, the existing vCenter Servers were re-pointed to those new external SSO systems. At the time, the recommendation was to have external SSO that would convert to PSC when you upgraded to vSphere 6.0. This recommendation was made for various reasons including Enhanced Linked Mode (ELM) and to better scale as the environment grew.

The Failure

The second phase became the longest working weekend of my life. The plan was to run an in-place upgrade for the external SSOs to upgrade them into vSphere 6.0 Platform Services Controllers. The project would then continue with a vCenter Server upgrade from 5.5 to 6.0. This was to be repeated at each site.

The procedure had been validated by performing the documented steps a month earlier in a less critical, non-production environment. Though the non-production environment was running the same vSphere version, it had a standalone vCenter Server, and Linked Mode was not involved. The upgrade on the non-production environment went smoothly, so I felt confident there was not going to be any problem with the production sites. Wrong!

On the night of the upgrade, I disabled monitoring for all involved systems, stopped the SRM and vCenter services and took a snapshot for each VM (4 External SSOs and 4 vCenter Servers). I verified that the latest SQL database backups had completed successfully the night before, and mounted the required ISO on each of the virtual machines. I started the upgrade at the biggest and most important site and everything worked flawlessly. I felt good about how things were proceeding and was ready to upgrade the other three locations.

Instead of performing the upgrade one site at a time and gradually bringing them back online, without thinking much about it, I kicked off the upgrade tasks concurrently for the remaining three SSO systems. The sites were basically isolated because services were not running and the tasks were exactly the same, so what could go wrong? After the external PSCs were completed, I moved on to vCenter and again initiated the upgrade tasks almost concurrently for the remaining three servers. What I had not anticipated was that as they came back online almost simultaneously, all services started automatically and the PSC replication partners were out of sync after the upgrade.

When all systems were upgraded and back online each of the sites was accessible, but Enhanced Linked Mode was not functioning. Logging in to any site did not show consistent results. The single pane of glass that should have displayed all four vCenter Servers never displayed more than two of them. A few reboots were performed, but nothing changed.

A support ticket was logged. I thought that an engineer would help me find and fix the issue before the maintenance window closed. This was wishful thinking on my part. While the engineer was being assigned, I was thinking that if the support engineer cannot fix it quickly, I would just revert everything to the snapshots I had taken before starting the upgrades.

When the support engineer called I explained the situation and the steps I had taken. The support engineer looked at the logs for the different PSCs and noticed discrepancies for replication partners and erroneous or incomplete entries in the database for those partners. I asked him how that could have happened and he said:

> "This is a bit uncommon, but I think I can fix it. Just give me a moment while I look for the right commands to add the additional replication partners, and then we will just restart the services and it should be good."

He did not really answer my question, but he made me feel like he knew what he was talking about so I decided to wait and let him work. After all, all eight systems had completed their upgrades without reporting any errors and we were just a few commands and a service restart away from completion.

The upgrade work had started after-hours on a Friday and it was almost midnight, the time I thought I would be reporting successful completion to my manager. I felt like I was just a block away from finishing a marathon. There was no point in thinking about going back because completion was so close. Whatever was wrong should be easy to repair....

The support engineer continued looking into things and then asked if he had permission to run the commands to add the missing replication partners. I told him to go ahead. I trusted the support engineer because he sounded very confident, knowledgeable, and he had done his research. He even stated that he had done these types of PSC corrections in the past and had validated the changes with colleagues after the corrections. We had a WebEx session going, and he had keyboard and mouse control. The support engineer typed the commands into Notepad first because we both wanted to review them before copying and pasting them to the terminal. The command syntax was long with username, password, FQDNs, and other values. Plus, we needed to run them in the other PSCs as well, with variations for server names.

The support engineer executed a few commands on the first affected system and everything seemed fine, but partner replication was still not occurring correctly. More checking of logs, more commands, and still no fix. I asked if he really thought we were on the right path and close to resolution, and he confidently said yes. Before we knew it, another three hours had gone by and we still had not resolved the issue. It was early morning and I was tired, and though I did not want to, reverting to snapshots looked like the best solution at that point. I told the support engineer:

> "I am calling it. Let us revert to the snapshots and go back to 5.5."

> And the support engineer said, "It is your call, but if you give me a little more time, I can fix it."

I insisted, stating that I was tired and would prefer to revert changes instead of continuing to attempt fixes.

> The support engineer replied, "Okay. Did you create a snapshot for all your systems, including the SQL servers?"
>
> "I did not take a snapshot of SQL servers, why would I need to do that?"
>
> And he responded, "The upgrade also upgraded the actual database, and you have to restore the database from backup because now they are not compatible."

Reverting to snapshots would not be as simple as I had thought. The vCenter databases were now incompatible with 5.5. I had validated the backups, but they were from the night before the upgrade. Even if we restored, the changes and all events from the workday would be lost! Realizing the situation, I asked the support engineer to keep troubleshooting. We both felt close to resolution, and I thought that at any moment he would find the problem, get it fixed, and then the upgrade (and fix) would be done. Of course, I had been thinking that for hours....

More hours passed and there was not much I could do. I watched the support engineer review logs and try different things, jump to another site to correlate and review more logs, and then try a few other things. It was almost dawn on Saturday and I was exhausted, so I decided to take a break and resume troubleshooting later. I emailed my manager with the details of what had occurred and said that we were close to finding and correcting the issue, and just needed more time after resting for a while. Although the maintenance window had passed, we needed to continue working, a situation that was strongly discouraged by the organization, even for weekend work. My manager stated that he would take the heat for allowing me to perform changes after the maintenance window and asked me to continue troubleshooting and provide him with updates.

I got back on the phone with the same support engineer early the next morning. The support engineer and I agreed to continue working together because of our knowledge of the environment and the issue. He was willing to work outside his shift and start early that day. Maybe he liked the challenge and wanted to be the one to resolve it. He was dedicated to customer success!

My manager told me that an exemption had been granted, without the need of an emergency change request, to allow us to keep working. All I had to do was either announce when things were fixed or provide an update every few hours. I spent 13 hours with the engineer that Saturday and about 10 more hours on Sunday. At one point the support engineer admitted that he had made a mistake that may have corrupted the database for one of the PSCs, but we kept going until the issue was resolved.

In the end, it was concluded that the mistake was running the upgrades on the PSCs concurrently. When they came back online, things were broken. The PSC with the corrupted database had to be rebuilt, and the resolution was to completely remove all replication partners from all PSCs and build their replication from scratch. After many weekend hours, the upgrade was completed after all the amends were performed.

How It Impacted My Customer

Believe it or not, the impact was not major. The infrastructure was still running and all of the customer's virtual machines were healthy and accessible. We had lost the ability to manage all vCenter servers together, but that only affected the virtualization team and some developers. It was not a big deal, though there may have been some pride involved as we did not want to report that the upgrade failed. Work could still be done, though the end result was not the desired state.

On a personal note, I was stubborn. Feeling so close to completing a rather simple upgrade, and encountering problems so close to the finish line, made me feel powerless and frustrated and I did not want to give up.

What Could I Have Done Differently?

There were several things I could have done differently.

- I should have done more research into upgrading an environment that used Linked Mode.
- I should have upgraded one site at the time. I erroneously assumed that because all sites were identical and "isolated" the concurrent upgrades would go perfectly.
- I could have been better prepared with the SQL databases, and ideally, should have taken backups just before the start of the upgrade instead of 24 hours earlier.
- Finally, I should not have anticipated that technical support engineers have magic wands that can quickly fix things. They are also human and can struggle with technical problems and make mistakes, as we all do.

What Did I Learn?

I learned a lot about PSC replication partners and how to validate their status. I now take more time to perform major tasks, do more research, open proactive tickets to inquire about known issues, ask colleagues and participate in the vCommunity to see if anyone has performed the action I am planning, and try to find the issues before performing the work.

Anything that can go wrong will go wrong, no matter how unlikely it may seem. Always have a contingency plan.

Do Not Neglect the Conceptual Layer

The Conceptual Layer, or Conceptual Model, provides a starting point to a design. It provides a non-technical description.

Over the years I have been called to lead complex support escalations on countless occasions and it never ceases to amaze me that, when I ask for documentation such as a detailed design document, no one can provide anything useful or anything at all! Ultimately, a lack of documentation often prolongs the time it takes to resolve an escalation by hours, days, or even for weeks in very large-scale, complex environments.

The Failure

The environment was fairly simple. It had a primary storage layer deployed across two sites connected with high speed, reliable WAN links. Snapshots were taken at each site and replicated bi-directionally.

There were issues with sizing, backup and secondary storage, performance, capacity, and stability.

Sizing Issues

After discussing the situation with the support organization, customer, and partner, it became clear that the environment was being used well beyond what it was designed for. This is not uncommon and can be caused by many factors such as failing to:

- Gather and document a customer's requirements, risks, constraints, and assumptions.
- Clearly document what the solution is designed to deliver and its limits.
- Implement the infrastructure according to the design specifications.
- Validate the implementation using a predefined, and approved, test plan.

Natural growth of a customer's business is also a common cause of an infrastructure being overused.

Backup and Secondary Storage Issues

It is generally well understood that to have sufficient data protection (backup) a production environment should keep at least three copies of data, two copies on different media and one copy offsite. In this case, I believe a misunderstanding in the conceptual model and logical design led to an incorrectly implemented environment. The infrastructure that was deployed lacked a backup solution and secondary storage, which led to the overuse of primary storage despite the design calling for a third-party backup solution with secondary storage.

This environment only used snapshots, on primary storage, with a single copy replicated to a DR site. Snapshots are commonly mistaken for backups. This resulted in the customer only having a total of two copies of data, with both copies on the same storage platform. No matter what vendor or product is used, despite claims to the contrary, it is a significant risk to not have a copy of your data on a different platform or media. A better approach could be primary storage (vendor X) and secondary storage (vendor Y) with offsite on tape via (vendor Y or Z). If all copies are maintained using a single vendor, there are no usable data copies when the vendor has a software issue. This can result in total data loss. This is rare, but cannot be ignored.

So, the infrastructure was deployed running mission-critical applications with a fundamental conceptual design issue where only two copies of data exist and both reside on primary storage, across two sites and on a single vendor's platform.

Performance, Capacity, and Stability Issues

Aside from the conceptual design issue, the customer also suffered performance, capacity and stability issues as a result of the storage layer not being designed to concurrently support primary and secondary storage as well as disaster recovery functions. Had it been designed to support these roles concurrently, it would likely have needed significantly more hardware and even then, conceptually, it would not be advisable.

The support organization reviewed logs, found various issues, got the environment back online and relatively stable, and got the customer back into production despite an extended outage. Then, a recommendation was made to upgrade the flash layer (capacity) along with the usual steps to bring the infrastructure up to the latest firmware, BIOS, and storage layer versions. How does the proposed solution address the performance, capacity and stability issues?

More flash (by way of swapping to larger capacity SSDs) means more data fits in the "hot" tier so this could help improve performance, but only if the previous flash tier was overutilized. This was not clear, but as the infrastructure was performing secondary storage and backup functionality with significant frequency and retention schedules, reducing or removing this activity would likely have a very positive effect on performance and capacity.

Upgrading firmware and BIOS might also help. Simple infrastructure maintenance does resolve issues, but in this case it did not directly address the customer's issues or the conceptual design problems. These upgrades were unlikely to be anything more than good practice for BAU (business as usual) maintenance to be performed.

What does the solution not address? The infrastructure's conceptual design has a significant flaw regarding data protection because the primary storage was being used for primary, secondary, and disaster recovery, as well as long term retention. Additionally, the customer only had two copies of data. Even if a product is capable of performing all of the required functions, it is not wise to use it exclusively as it creates a single point of failure.

The recommended solution arguably put the customer in a riskier situation because they may think that upgrading the flash layer and firmware resolved the issue, and would continue to use and possibly grow the environment in a way that is not advisable. This could potentially set them up for future failures on a larger scale.

What Could I Have Done Differently?

There are several things I would do differently.

- Perform a current state assessment and better understand the problem.
- Review the conceptual design. If the design documentation does not exist, review the environment at the conceptual layer.

  Find out if documentation exists before a disaster. If documentation does not exist or if it is not high quality, bring it up to standard. And if you do not have the time or skills and experience to do it yourself, raise the issue with your manager and engage an experienced Enterprise Architect to assist.
- Review if the implementation aligns with the proposed logical and physical design layers.

If the environment is conceptually flawed, create a conceptual design and put forward a recommendation. In this case, my recommendation at the conceptual layer would be to design and implement a secondary storage layer with a third-party backup solution.

If the conceptual design is viable, move on to the logical and physical layers. Compare the current state assessment with the design, and/or against the known requirements of the platform if the infrastructure design or requirements are not known. Gather these as part of the assessment as no recommendations can be made without first understanding what needs to be achieved.

In this case, the customer's current environment was largely suitable to support their primary storage requirements even after adding a secondary storage layer with a third-party backup solution. However, the migration/interim state also needs to be considered.

How Would I Address the Issues?

The environment needed a backup and secondary storage solution, and was also impacted by performance, capacity, and stability issues. It was being used well beyond what it was designed for. I would perform the following steps to address the customer's issues:

Perform "back of the napkin" sizing to get a feel for whether the infrastructure is sized appropriately. If it is not, dive deeper and identify and document where the sizing fails.

What would be required to scale the infrastructure (if possible) to support the current (and future) workloads?

1. Identify what workload/s can be migrated off if the solution cannot be scaled. In this case, removing some snapshots allowed the customer's environment to remain stable long enough to properly design and implement the secondary storage and third-party backup solution.
2. Document a scalable and repeatable model to accommodate natural growth over time. This helps the customer understand what the infrastructure is capable of today and the thresholds (for example, capacity) at which it needs to be scaled, along with the limits of the infrastructure.
3. Design and implement a secondary storage layer with a third-party backup solution.
4. Make sure that the designed backup strategy (frequency and retention) is performed and test restorations are validated before making any changes to the primary storage layers. Perform general infrastructure maintenance on the primary storage layer at the disaster recovery site including BIOS, firmware and any hardware (for example, SSD) upgrades.
5. Perform full operational verification of the DR site.
6. Perform general infrastructure maintenance on the primary storage layer at the primary site including BIOS, firmware and any hardware (for example, SSD) upgrades.
7. Perform full operational verification of the primary site.

What Did I Learn?

I learned several things from this experience.

- If the infrastructure has a conceptual, logical, or physical design issue, address that issue specifically. Do not try to throw hardware at the problem.
- Review the infrastructure design and scope, compare it to the current state, and document any differences such as workload, size, make/model, snapshot quantity, and retention.
- Perform "back of the napkin" sizing to get a feel for whether the environment is properly sized or not.

Architecting for a War Zone

Have you ever considered having to architect a solution in a war zone?! Not a typical scenario, but you could find yourself in such a situation and you might have to design for it.

This story is not about a failure, but this engagement posed an unusual challenge and resulted in valuable lessons learned. The challenge was tied to Business Continuity and Disaster Recovery (BCDR).

The Project

In this engagement, the client mission was to engage with all businesses in their country to host their workloads, and to carry on and endure even during the worst times and under the most rigorous conditions. Think of it as a country-wide business continuity and disaster recovery plan.

Usually the Statement of Work (SOW) identifies the general things that need to be accomplished and the contractual limits, but you do not know everything about the customer or what they need from the SOW. After the SOW was accepted, I was introduced to the PM (Project Manager) and the project began.

At the first internal project kickoff meeting, the customer name was revealed and discussions started. I had many mixed feelings about this engagement: What are these people (the customer) thinking? They are in a war zone! People are actually dying there!

Higher Purpose

It is sometimes difficult for engineers to comprehend things from the sales perspective. In our line of work it is hard to find purpose other than helping customers to achieve their business and technical goals. I seek reasons beyond the financial element because it motivates me and gives me a higher purpose. For example, if you work on an engagement for a healthcare-related project you may help the healthcare provider's business, but I would like to think that because of the work we do, we are also making someone's life better.

I felt that this delivery would help people carry on with their lives in a time of crisis by ensuring that the customer's services were up and running. That was my higher purpose…this was the edge I needed.

The Customer Team

Because of the delicacy of the situation, we needed to make sure that the design workshops were highly productive, and we held a series of remote conference calls and sessions to gather requirements to build our conceptual model. I got to hear the names and recognize the voices of people on the customer team. Their team was very professional, knew what they wanted, and were on top of their game.

I think we are lucky when we meet a customer with a strong team that has total alignment and coherence, and very good technical knowledge. Why lucky? Well, not because this makes our lives easier. On the contrary, it makes things more difficult because expectations are high and the desired outcome is very well defined. But, it is lucky because you are challenged, you get to go beyond the conventional, and you get to explore options, workarounds, extreme design decisions, and topics that you might have not have thought about before. You can learn from such customers as you share your knowledge with them. It is a thing of beauty.

Commitment and Process

I arrived the day before the design workshops, prepared the initial conceptual design, and was ready to venture wherever this project would lead. The next day, I expected to sit with all of the stakeholders and get things going. When I entered into the conference room I found myself standing in front of over 20 people. I was not expecting that many people. However, the large number of participants relayed a positive message about interest in this project.

The attendees were all stakeholders in the initiative, including business people, architects, administrators, support engineers, and security operations personnel. On some projects you have to fight with project managers to make the needed attendees available for different meetings, and you end up flipping calendar appointments and adjourning sessions until you can get the right combination of people. Not here! All hands were at the table, all stakeholders were there, and everyone wanted to understand everything even if it was not part of their role. This was complete commitment, and it gave me even more reason to push boundaries.

Because of the turmoil and uncertainty in the region they were accustomed to treating everything as if they were the only people responsible for the solutions, and they validated and approved everything on the spot.

For me, this translated into:

- Conducting design workshops in daytime.
- Writing the design document at night.
- Reviewing the design document the next morning with the customer.
- Validating certain points ad-hoc in my lab environment.

Note: When delivering design documents, there is a framework to be followed, but there may be variations. How is this determined? It must be based on the customer's attitude, engagement, and willingness to level up the framework to have it produce its best results.

For example, in education, training is normally delivered by an instructor and the instructor has a curriculum to follow. The class is more interesting if all attendees are well versed in the prerequisites and the topic at hand; then, the instructor can go above and beyond. But, if everyone is new to the topic, the instructor must slow the pace, and proceed in smaller steps. In both scenarios the curriculum is followed and the class gets delivered, but the personal gain and outcome are different.

Requirements and Solutions

Today, technology and communication are as important for survival as food and water. We can no longer tolerate the absence of the digital infrastructure.

This was not a normal design and architecture. Architecting for a war zone posed unusual, extreme risk scenarios. All failure scenarios were on the table and every single one of them needed to be mitigated. All of them!

We looked at various scenarios:

- What if a rocket hit the datacenter?
- What if the datacenter was raided?
- What if the electrical power went out?
- What if the administration workstations get a security breach?
- What if we have no access to the datacenter for a long period of time?
- What if the IT team was lost (unable to participate in operations or recovery)?

We were literally designing for failure! Operations and performance were still important, but availability and recoverability were the primary goals we had to address, in addition to some heavy lifting when it came to operability.

The biggest problem was that hardware procurement required six months, so we had to work with whatever they had in their datacenters. We did not buy anything new so, in effect, all hardware was a constraint. They had fairly new hardware, but we needed to review the details and verify things worked as required.

To achieve the required BCDR, we first had to identify all of the single points of failure, and mitigate them with something viable that could be tested. Their current setup was subject to change based on the outcome of the design workshops as long as it did not involve getting new hardware.

Going through their existing setups, we had to determine what we could use or reuse to achieve a certain requirement, mitigate its risks, and minimize the changes required so that it did not disrupt other operations.

After 14 rigorous days we produced an architecture document and a low-level technical document. Everyone was onsite and we were doing daily reviews, so it was immediately approved. We performed a full 14-hour design review on the last day as well.

The biggest changes involved:

- Splitting the environments into different datacenter halls (compute, storage and network).
- Splitting the halls into different functionality (production, staging/development, and recovery).
- Splitting the recovery into two stages (on-premises, off-premises).
- Splitting into three teams (onsite, offsite, with rotation across sites). Reworking the BC and DR plans (even during the worst of times you still have an SLA to deal with).

What Could I Have Done Differently?

To be honest, I would not change anything. This experience taught me so much, especially about the importance of people and process.

The biggest constraint was existing hardware as it limited the customer's ability to incorporate workloads as easily as they would have liked. Given more time hardware could have been obtained that would have enabled further optimization, but it was not possible to upgrade the hardware in the allotted time.

What Did I Learn?

I learned a lot from this engagement. Sometimes, you go to the desert with no means of survival and you have only your wits and willingness to survive. This is how it felt to me on this project.

On another note, having a very knowledgeable customer is lucky, but it can also be a nightmare. In this project, they were very demanding, in a very tiring way, both technically and with their timelines. Under different circumstances perhaps the timeline could have been less aggressive. Given the size and scope of this project it would normally have taken 40 days, not the 14 days that I was allocated.

It is not technology itself that saves the day; it is the people who build and operate the technology so that it can survive various conditions, be they business, technical, or hostile environments such as war. People and process are very tricky aspects in any engagement. Do not presume anything about the customer before you meet them, even if internal information has been shared. The sales or presales team usually engages with about 30% of the customer team and might base their assumptions on what they learn from those people. The other 70% of people involved when the engagement begins are a complete unknown area to explore, and identifying and connecting with them is part of the skill set needed in steering a delivery. As an architect, profile the users and other stakeholders, and align your discussions in a way that meets their expectations. Customers should feel that you are dedicated to each and every one of them and understand their area of interest.

Always put yourself in the customer's shoes. This means getting involved with their process and convincing yourself the proposed design is optimal even before trying to convince the customer. As architects, we are meant to be the trusted consultants and advisors to our customers. We need to know what is at stake for the customer and understand where they are coming from to be able to provide relevant answers and solutions, not just because they seem technically valid. For example, sometimes deadlines are forced by other dependent projects, while other deadlines are forced because of hardware end of life or even software end of life. It is very important to bear the customer's issues so that they feel as if you are providing the kind of service that you yourself would want. This builds a whole new level of unbreakable trust.

In a perfect world, things would always go smoothly and you would have the ability to do almost anything. However, architects do not exist in a perfect world! Our role is to deal with reality and engage the problems of our customers. We take whatever is given and make it as good as possible given the circumstances.

What is Mission Critical?

What is mission critical? I have been an IT architect and technical leader for decades and this question has come up frequently through the years. It sometimes seems like so many things have been classified as mission critical that the term has lost its meaning. That is not to say that a function or application is not critical to a business or infrastructure, but the classification has been applied so broadly that truly mission critical operations can be obscured or impacted by lessor priorities that claim equal importance. "It is email; of course it is mission critical!"

This problem often occurs because:

- The business and IT think everything is mission critical.
- IT often does not know what is most important, treating the print server and the DHCP server with as much importance as the CRM or ERP system.

This was the case at ITAR. They did not even create Service Level Agreements (SLAs) because *everything* was important and had to be returned to service immediately upon failure! This, despite the fact that ITAR was a military command running an operational theater of war and conducted critical missions where lives were at stake and actions could have international consequences. In this chaotic environment troubleshooting and ticket management had become the predominant activities while uptime suffered. Someone needed to take a step back and define what was really mission critical, and what was needed to stabilize the environment.

The Failure

With over 1000 datacenters running countless applications, everyone was a customer, and everything was a priority, so nothing was a priority. There were command centers within command centers at joint, regional, and local levels, with different organizations operating different parts tied to different contracts and different missions, some handled by military and others by civilian contractors and subcontractors.

When I arrived at ITAR everything was on fire, and everyone was a fireman. Every hour of every day, everyone focused their attention on putting out the latest fires that often spread from infrastructure to infrastructure, application to application, circuit to circuit, and so forth. Everyone was so busy putting out fires that no-one had taken time to step back and understand why there were so many issues, and look into solutions. Some recommendations had been made, but they applied only to parts of the environment and were largely ignored. The constant onslaught of issues had resulted in an operational uptime average of only 30%!

The Mission Takes Precedence

Everything was a priority, so nothing was a priority, but there were extremely important exceptions. This was an operational theater of war, so operations could include rescues, attacks, surveillance, RECON, and "special" missions. These clearly were critical missions and took precedence over all other operations, functions, maintenance, and other activities. But, problems occurred when critical missions had to work around these other activities, and when other activities were disrupted as a result of a critical mission. A 30% operational uptime average was completely unacceptable.

Take a Step Back and Review Everything

Uptime was not only important to the mission but was fundamental to the planning, management, and operations of everything within the environment. What was causing the problems with uptime and the impact on ITAR operations? What could be done about it?

This is where I became active in my role as a technical leader and architect. Having a broad understanding of how all of the pieces of an infrastructure connect and interconnect, I took a step back and reviewed both the environment and the issues together.

- What problems have been occurring most frequently? Are these problems isolated to a particular location or infrastructure?
- What is the frequency of these problems? What steps have been taken to resolve them?
- Is the resolution consistent? How much can be automated or eliminated?
- Do problems stem from configuration errors or bad practices?

Much more went into the review process, but these were some of the fundamental questions I asked while taking a step back and looking at things. There were some key takeaways from this research and analysis.

Trust Nothing, Verify Everything

There is a well-known admonishment, "Trust but verify." This is fine if you trust that the correct decisions were made, the correct configurations were set, and the correct best practices were followed. Initially, when I found a mistake such as an incorrect value on a Maximum Transmission Unit (MTU) setting on a network adapter or storage adapter, I would check the rest of the nodes in the cluster to verify that everything was configured the same way. But there was little time to do things properly, so that practice had to be abandoned.

Imagine a world where you have hundreds or thousands of clusters and most of them have a uniform set of hardware, applications, services and so forth. They should all follow a similar set of best practices and set their configuration correspondingly. However, that was not the case at ITAR. When you have a dispersed infrastructure spread over geographic geopolitical boundaries, originally configured by one organization, and then managed and operated by an unrelated organization, mistakes will happen….

We defined the best practices that should be applied as uniformly as possible on every cluster, at every location, for each of the applications. This was not difficult to do, but no-one had done it until now, to the detriment of the infrastructure and its uptime.

Best practices were established, MTUs were set, storage policy was established, virtual machine memory and CPU allocations were defined, and application configurations and performance was aligned to the needs of the application (as opposed to the demands of the end-users). Most importantly, Role-Based Access Control (RBAC) was enforced on a *need to access* basis, not a *want to access* basis. Everyone does not need to be an administrator!

That is Not the Way We Do It

Initially, we encountered serious pushback to our attempts to modernize and revolutionize the way things were being done. The common response was, "That is not the way we are used to doing it," or "This is the way we did it yesterday, so this is the way we will do it tomorrow." People had gotten so used to doing what they had always done that they had grown complacent and were only comfortable doing things that way.

This was an operational theater of war, so when someone in authority says, "This is how we do it," they expect you to comply. They did not expect to hear, "No. We are not going to do that anymore because it is wrong and does not work," but that is what we told them. This was a shock to many people, but we prevailed.

Success after success built up in a very short period of time. People took notice and stopped questioning and trying to block the actions being taken, which proved to be a win for everyone involved.

Success

We were successful! Clusters stopped running out of space and crashing on a daily or hourly basis. Applications stopped starving out other pieces of the infrastructure, causing cascading failures. Weird problems caused by minute configuration failures stopped occurring. It was a fundamental shift in the operation and functioning of the infrastructure.

Uptime was no longer measured as 33.33333% or an "average of 30% uptime." We achieved 100% operational uptime, a new record that persisted for 600+ days in this active, highly critical infrastructure.

Time to Innovate and Optimize

The phones were not ringing off the hook. The queues were no longer filled with critical infrastructure failure tickets. With firefighting reduced to a manageable level, time was freed up for the architects and engineers to innovate and optimize the environment like never before. External "agencies" started visiting us, interested in modeling their infrastructures after ours. For ITAR, this was a golden age of communication and collaboration.

The most important recipients of our operational success were the mission-critical operations that were being executed on a regular basis. These missions were no longer prone to problems or failure due to infrastructure issues, and a more streamlined and optimized environment supported greater levels of success. This literally saved lives, which was very rewarding.

What Did I Learn?

Coming from an Enterprise background, an environment like this might be intimidating or overwhelming. But, when you come to a project with Agile principles, and apply defined and refined best practices, you can make significant changes and steer an organization in a positive direction to success.

Some organizations use the term *mission critical* with little regard for what it really means, and do not prioritize operations appropriately relative to more important missions. Some missions, such as the war-related operations at ITAR, are truly mission critical. Missions that involve life and death decisions or have potentially far-reaching consequences are certainly more critical than others, and must be clearly defined as mission critical and given the highest priority. By understanding your customer's mission, regardless of whether they are a small business or a large Enterprise, you should be able to identify the truly mission-critical operations in their environment.

Absent Stakeholders and Missing Requirements

Right from the beginning it seemed like the project would be one to remember. My customer kicked off a major Virtual Desktop Infrastructure (VDI) project that would provide significant benefits to their business but, by the time the project wrapped up, it was memorable because of the lessons that could be applied to future large-scale projects.

The Project

My customer had adopted VDI technology for some of their users, but like any large company, they had started to suffer from environment sprawl and the technical debt that came with it. One implementation had turned into two, and two had turned into four. They were using two different VDI technologies and all of the environments were outdated and out of support. They had a user base of around 2000 users across all the environments, and these environments played a critical role in delivering key business applications and processes.

The goal was to deliver a single environment utilizing a single vendor. Because they were working with multiple environments and multiple vendors, we positioned a series of workshops to help decide on a vendor and architecture. Over a few months, we met with the project team multiple times, helped them select their platform, and created a design and implementation timeline to meet their goals. The effort to complete the plan was put into a Statement of Work and submitted, along with the design.

And then the challenges first started appearing....

The Failure

The customer had an aggressive timeline for completing the implementation to meet business requirements, mostly around funding and end-of-year change windows, and they were also asking for onboarding and migration assistance. The timeline that we agreed to relied on fast approval through their internal architecture and procurement processes. The environment builds would only take a few months, and the remaining time would be used to prepare and migrate users and applications.

Though architectural approval was quick, the Statement of Work was held up in procurement. This delay cost three months that had been scheduled for deploying the platform and the customer did not adjust their project timeline or scope because deadlines were imposed by other business rules. However, this was not an insurmountable problem as we were able to make up a lot of time during the deployment phase.

As we moved into the migration planning phase, we ran into another problem. The customer team for this project owned the existing VDI environments. They were part of the Datacenter Infrastructure team, and their leadership had signed off on the project. However, End-User Computing (EUC) solutions are not just datacenter projects. They involve people from other parts of the IT organization such as desktop management and applications, and these other teams had not been included or made available during the workshop.

To meet business requirements around disaster recovery, the design called for using non-persistent desktops and new application delivery tools. When the Desktop (EUC) team was finally brought into the project to talk about desktop images, they objected to using different application delivery technology. The design had cleared architecture, so there should not have been a problem. But…that was not the case.

They had not validated the technology or evaluated the impacts that it would have on other components in the environment, and they had not developed a workflow or determined who would do the work. Frustrations mounted as the implementation turned into a political football.

The Desktop team ultimately said that they would not use the new application delivery technology. Management backed them, and we were told to find a new path forward.

The Solution

The lack of the new application delivery technology torpedoed our design as we were unable to meet the disaster recovery (DR) requirements that the customer had dictated. All migration and implementation planning activities were put on hold while key portions of the solution were re-architected and re-implemented. This included using a different provisioning model for virtual desktops.

We reviewed the new plans with the Desktop team, and they agreed to the new approach. We were finally given approval to implement the new architecture and perform a DR test to validate it.

After the DR test was successfully completed and we were able to resume migration planning, the window for completing the migration had narrowed to a few weeks. The customer, realizing that their vision could not be fully completed in the remaining time, limited the scope of the migration work and dropped some parts of the project. With these changes agreed to and in place, the migration work proceeded, and all of the required users were migrated to the new environment by the customer's required end date.

How It Impacted My Customer

My customer was unable to achieve their original vision. Their plan to consolidate multiple virtual desktop environments into one new environment and decommission the old environments was put on hold. Only some of the virtual desktops were migrated, and everything else was postponed for a later date.

Rearchitecting the solution had financial impacts as well. Additional storage was required to meet the disaster recovery requirements after the architecture change, and this had to be procured and charged against the project.

What Could I Have Done Differently?

I did not realize until the workshop phase had already begun that the Desktop team was not represented. The Datacenter Infrastructure team we worked with was familiar with VDI as they managed the current VDI environments, but it is not uncommon for the VDI and Desktop teams to be separate.

Had I realized that someone from the Desktop team was not going to be present during the scheduling phase, I would have insisted that they attend, even if it meant moving the workshop date to accommodate them. VDI projects need representation from multiple teams, including the Desktop team, so that all of the requirements can be defined. I missed key requirements and details about the environment because the Desktop team was not present.

There were other opportunities to get the Desktop team involved in the project before starting migration planning, such as the design review at the beginning of the project. These were missed opportunities, and we ended up having to do rework because of it.

As delays mounted and pushed back the start of the desktop migrations, I should have set more realistic expectations with the customer about how much we could accomplish. When it became clear that the architecture needed to change, the migration scope should have been reduced to make sure that it could be accomplished. However, this did not happen until the last minute.

What Did I Learn?

End-User Computing projects require stakeholders from multiple areas within the enterprise IT organization. By not including key stakeholders, I had provided a design that relied upon components that parts of the organization would not support. This required a costly design change and reimplementation that impacted the migration time.

As an architect, it is important to be aware of the key players who can impact the project and make sure that they are included. When consulting on a project identify the key players early on. This may require working with the customer's project team and your sales team.

It is also important to understand the political impacts of introducing new technologies and new concepts into an organization. New technologies can solve business challenges, but they can also change team workloads and workflows. This can introduce new blockers from teams that do not want to reallocate resources or change their processes. You cannot rely just on the strength of the technology solution that you are proposing or implementing. You must show how it provides value to the business while being sensitive to the needs of the team.

How to Win Big in Uncertainty

I am a pre-sales architect and this story revolves around our efforts to deliver an IT and workforce transformation solution to one of the largest insurance companies in a region. We were able to close this deal, but the experience was cumbersome and required 24 weeks of tireless effort.

Working with any global customer brings with it unique perspectives and challenges for an architect. This includes dealing with highly critical systems, old and rigid processes, and last but not least, legacy systems. Cultural adaptability is another major challenge as we live in a diverse global environment and it is important to account for culture and get along well with your stakeholders. Never underestimate the nuances of any of these elements if you want success with any of the industry verticals.

Opportunity Background

For most C-level executives, a typical workforce transformation project outcome is all about raising employee skills and productivity through an enhanced digital experience, all within a reasonable timeframe, and within bounds of a finite and ever-shrinking IT budget.

We were tasked to digitize a 50-year-old company. The company had around 1500 retail offices across the country and served approximately 15 million customers. Such a large customer base has a big IT footprint, involving 10 primary vendors, with four datacenters, 500+ servers, 10,000 end points, 1000s of peripherals, and so on.

We approached the project hastily as we were competing against an incumbent vendor whose contract renewal was due in just a few weeks. The customer was set to renew the contract if they decided to do business as usual and not do a digital transformation. Our sales team sniffed out this opportunity and proposed to change the game by introducing our approach to the new digital workplace. Immediately after the first client meeting a pilot was proposed with a 40-branch roll-out.

This was not an easy project to execute, especially as a pre-sales team with limited assistance from any partner and no dedicated professional services support. A lot of risk was involved because it touched production environments. I should have been more diligent on these aspects.

As the lead architect, I was responsible for streamlining delivery of the overall project. I had to give the project a structure for better execution. A framework was necessary, so I applied my tried and tested approach to segment the opportunity into the following areas:

- Technology.
- People.
- Process.

Technology

Because it was a pilot in a production environment, choosing a release was always part of my plan (N-1 is my go-to rule for version selection). However, we were competing with an incumbent vendor, and we had to propose the latest and greatest versions with full features to differentiate us from other vendors. Desperate times call for desperate measures, and despite the risk I had to give in if we wanted our new digital workplace initiative to stand any chance against the competition. VMware products in our BOM (Bill of Materials) included Horizon 6, AirWatch, vSphere 6, NSX 6, vRA 6.2, vROPS, and more), and were all new releases competing against a tried and tested Citrix portfolio.

We were also asked to repurpose some old desktops instead of replacing and buying new thin clients. This was never tested, so it was not going to be approved by our management, and I was uncomfortable with this idea, which set us up for failure. Our competition was willing to do this, as they had experience with legacy clients and supported repurposed desktops.

Our initial reaction was resistance and frustration, but my sales team thought out of the box and came up with a proposal to replace the old desktops with a new vendor at a fraction of cost. The new vendor was asked to go through a TAP (Technical Alliance Program) certification before its hardware could be added into the HCL (Hardware Compatibility List), and with our help they decided to go forward as it gave them a new market to explore with low cost Linux thin clients. (This vendor now competes with larger and well-established players, and has been helpful in some very tight budget situations.)

Lessons learned: Always stay creative even in most difficult technical situations. There are companies willing to participate and contribute in a joint opportunity if you reach out and propose a plan. Success comes from most unexpected places and you never know until you try.

Another project requirement was to set up a self-service onboarding experience for Day 0 productivity. Micro-segmentation was also a security requirement and the ability to deliver it made us unique, so I added this to the overall solution design. I also added vROPS for its dashboarding, predictive analysis, and application-level visibility. This involved a 360-degree integration with the entire ecosystem, and had never been done before in my region.

As we had limited technical staff to put this into production, I collaborated with my global peers and specialized partner organizations.

People

Investing in people is critical to success of any project, especially people with high impact roles. That is the population to focus on first, and they can be both internal (peers) and external stakeholders (customer and partners). Although a workforce transformation ultimately affects the entire organization, some people's roles and skill sets are critical to achieving the highest-priority business outcomes right away.

We learned that people were the key to success if we wanted to replace an existing technology platform. When we tried to roll out our first few pilot users, we saw a lot of discomfort from end users who were, understandably, not accustomed to the new way of working. Connecting to VDI and logging into to a thin client was a major shift from using a desktop to store and access a file, and user ratings were poor on willingness to shift to new model. The solution was to use the most tech-savvy branch as pilot users, and this worked well (although I had to fly down to this site to get first hand feedback from the business). The tech-savvy users adopted the new technology more easily and related their positive experience to others.

Lessons Learned: Feedback and dialogue are very important. Most C-level initiatives fail to deliver on the business outcomes because end users are not open to the idea of change. Often the problem is lack of communication and failure to get users on board. As an architect it is important to look beyond technology and relate to the end users (business owners).

Another area was choice of partners to do integrations and onboarding of legacy platforms. A typical company might have approximately 20% legacy platforms, and you must plan to deal with them. I knew that if I researched it well I would find someone within the partner ecosystem who was handling legacy systems across the industry vertical. I interviewed some customer IT engineers and found information about a partner resource who was an expert in developing and integrating scanners with VDI systems. In early versions, VMware Horizon had very limited support for USB redirection and bandwidth requirements were very high on the legacy PCoIP protocol. Citrix always had a much wider support and compatibility, as they had tuned the platform and used a load balancer (NetScaler) to optimize bandwidth. However, with help from this dedicated partner and some adjustments to the VMware software, scanner firmware, and code base from our partner, we were able to produce better results, and our scans were better resolution, faster, and able to deal with very large files.

Last, was an ability to integrate the entire VMware portfolio to deliver Self-Service Desktop as a Service (DaaS) while including Citrix apps and RDSH apps together without major changes to the platform. This required collaborating with my friends and peers in the industry across the US and APJ, where such solutions had already been tried in POCs (Proofs of Concept). With help, and my team's willingness to work on weekends and learn how to do this, we were able to deliver the necessary IT outcome in four weeks.

Another important aspect as an architect is to remember post-deployment support. With companies such as VMware there is a robust support system that can help customers troubleshoot a complex system with many disparate components from many different vendors. Reach out to the right set of people in support who have experience with the complete portfolio. During the pilot we faced some product issues, but because I had friends in support due to past meetings with people at the company and community events such as VMUGs, we sailed through the issues we faced.

Lessons learned: The positive result was possible because of collaboration between people and technology. Keep legacy systems in mind and have an inclusion strategy to handle them as these are often business-critical applications that are used by many different users. Always make friends within your customer base, partners, and the companies you work for, and help others as you expect them to help you. It is a very small world and you get back what you serve.... Think karma!

Process

A complex project will always push you into a situation that could result in process violations. The main reasons for processes are to retain a formal structure and provide a well-defined framework for the overall execution of important procedural elements, and to avoid errors and maintain repeatability. As we tried to onboard more users and branches as part of this project, we increasingly faced process challenges. Some of the challenges, especially around security, were self-induced due to lack of proper planning.

When working with a large product set, each set requires different approaches to security exceptions around opening ports, user authorizations, and so on. We initially struggled getting changes approved because change management was a weekly process (it usually is for large customers), and the CAB (Change Advisory Board) was constantly dealing with emergency requests. Changes were not only deeply scrutinized and discouraged, but were often denied.

After constant head-butting, we comprehensively reviewed our solution and submitted a single change request that included business justifications with risks and remediation.

Some process violations were introduced by the customer because they wanted us to upgrade additional infrastructure components that were part of future implementations, but never part of the original plans. Initially, I was okay with this, but it caused major timeline shifts and we were already short of staff, so we had to politely ask for additional customer resources to perform those tasks while our team helped with technical procedures specific to the solution. Always leverage Installation and Planning guides to fast track the process and avoid reinventing the wheel.

Lessons Learned: As an architect, prepare in advance for change management and have a Plan B ready. Do not refuse or accept customer requests without analysis of effort and how it affects your timeline. Acting without analysis may cause you to lose out on an opportunity to make some friends and get to know the internal referees or advocates on whose behalf you are doing the work. At the same time be assertive and do not give up on timelines; this is a gentle balancing act you should be ready to do as a lead architect.

Last but not least, be aware of internal organizational constraints. Do not overcommit to the customer anything not supported by your parent organization. This avoids future pain and protects your credibility. The rule of thumb is to always check with peers and your management before falling into the trap of overcommitting.

We had many situations in this project where a technical requirement violated our internal processes and I had to politely deny, or creatively think of an alternate solution. Always document such issues because they may again become an issue in future.

What Could I Have Done Differently?

There were several areas where I could have done something differently.

- Prerequisites: I should have asked for additional staff to do the pilot run, even if it meant some investment from the management stakeholders. This would have freed up bandwidth from my team (which did a lot of work to speed up other tasks), and reduced the time needed to roll out the project. It would have also saved some weekends for the team, and allowed them to spend more time with family and friends
- Deployment: I should not have allowed a customer and sales teams to pressure me into a "big pilot" run with a tight timeline and no POC. If we had done a POC instead of hurrying to do a pilot the major risks could have been avoided. We were lucky to pull this project off, but as an experienced architect, I now always insist on identifying risks in advance to prevent future failures.
- Push Back: Yes, push back on the prerequisites and deployment, but also push back against the need to be on the latest and greatest version of software. To deliver a pilot solution on a first major release, accommodate customer requests to support legacy platforms, and make decisions based on competition rather than doing what is best for the platform; all posed risk. Winning is important, but highlighting the risks is far better than failing to deliver the solution because of risks that were not accounted for, or accepted despite being too risky

How It Impacted My Customer

My customer transformed to the region's first Digital Workplace among their vertical. As a result employee retention and productivity significantly improved. Being a digital enterprise, their bottom line had grown considerably, all thanks to the IT initiatives they took five years ago when they were one of the early adopters and gained a distinct business advantage. I am quite proud of my efforts, but wish that I could have done this in a shorter time frame. Hindsight is always 20/20....

What Did I Learn?

The story is still as relevant today as it was when I executed this project. Almost every organization will need to transform its IT and workforce in the future, and do so at a rapid pace. As an architect I am always aware that this type of initiative is big, complex, time consuming, and success is not guaranteed. Never give up!

Technological transformation, which is seen by some as a detriment to humans, becomes a vehicle for advancing an organization. If you can focus on the right path and framework, you, your employer, and your customers will be well prepared to face the future.

My team and I missed out on some elements during this project, and I will certainly apply the lessons learned for future projects. Your experience may vary as no two organizations have the same circumstances, and there is no single recipe to follow.

Follow the Process: It is Really Simple...

ITAR Corporation, a software development services provider, was working onsite at one of its financial customer locations. With several recent successful projects, ITAR had emerged from a troubled record of program execution for the customer, turned around the business relationship, and was winning new business. ITAR Corporation then won a large contract to build an enterprise application called FPS (Financial Processing System) from scratch for a newly formed business unit. ITAR formed the FPS project team with dedicated resources the week after being awarded the contract.

The ITAR FPS project team was comprised of Tim as delivery lead, Jade as project manager, Jim as business analyst, Peter as development leader, Sam in charge of quality control, and myself as the architect. In addition, there were five software developers and three testers on the team. Josh was the business owner from the financial customer.

On Friday I received an email invite to the kickoff meeting scheduled for the following Monday. I left work ready for the weekend and happy that I had been assigned a new project that was of critical importance for our customer.

The Failure

I drove into my office excited that the FPS project was kicking off. I picked up coffee at the barista, and greeted everyone as I entered the conference room —especially Josh, our customer. Jade started the overhead projector and shared her screen, presenting the project plan. I clearly recall Jade saying,

> "This is the project work breakdown structure. The important milestone date is six weeks from now, when we will have the FPS application deployed to production in the customer datacenter."

> Josh, the customer, then added, "Jade told me that your team is going to deploy on time and meet all our enterprise architecture and security requirements."
>
> To this Jade replied, "Yes. We are going to do that and will deliver in six weeks."

With that, the meeting ended, and Josh, Jade and Tim left the room.

Jim, Peter, Sam and I were still in the conference room with two developers. My mind was racing, wondering why Jade had said six weeks, but I put that on hold. I asked Jim whether he could share with the team the requirements for the Minimum Viable Product, including elements such as the use cases (epics and feature requests) and the personas (actors). The project was scheduled for delivery in six weeks and I had not seen any of the requirements. Peter and Sam seconded the request. Then, Jim said to us,

> "I know what you all are asking. I do not have any draft requirements yet. I still need to have discussions with Josh and his team and incorporate their inputs into my requirements draft, which I have not yet created. Following this I need to schedule a walkthrough of the requirements with all of you for clarifications, feasibility, and clarity, so you can consume the requirements. Following that I would schedule a signoff meeting with the customer and obtain customer signoff on the requirements."
>
> Having heard what Jim said, almost all of us said in chorus, "How did ITAR end up stating six weeks for a production-capable deliverable of the FPS software to the customer, without communicating with the software engineering team, and without considering inputs from architect and engineers about feasibility, design, and level of efforts?"

I had more questions. Who decided six weeks? Why? But, I did not raise these questions aloud. I went home worried about the situation and began thinking about how to adjust the plan and successfully complete this project.

I scheduled a meeting the next day with Tim and the entire ITAR FPS team. I did not include the customer, Josh.

The next day I drove into the office early, grabbed a double expresso from the barista, and was very composed. I had put together a mind map for the FPS project and was prepared for the meeting. As we met to discuss the FPS project, I started the meeting by thanking everyone for participating and then I said,

"I am afraid we have failed in following established processes even before we started this project. We have made our First Attempt In Learning (FAIL) on day one of the project itself." And with that I presented a FAIL slide.

The FAIL slide made the following points:

- Communication is broken.
- Scope of the project is not finalized.
- Requirements are not finalized.
- There is no Minimal Viable Product (MVP) version of requirements.
- The interfaces of FPS are unknown.
- Performance requirements are unknown.
- Level of Effort cannot be determined.
- The Project is delayed and will not be completed in six weeks.

After I completed the slide, Tim mentioned that high-level requirements were known, based on the contract award, and the team had to move forward with a six-week deliverable timeline because Josh had committed this schedule to the new business unit head. Everyone recognized that we had to acknowledge what had happened and take this as an opportunity to move forward anyway. We put together an action plan to move forward, and we began execution per the new project plan.

Jade had mentioned to the team that it was Josh who wanted the project to be done in six weeks, a record timeframe. Later on, as the project progressed, we found out that Jade had used a project plan that had not been reviewed by the team, but it had been baselined and committed to the customer's project server. That is where Josh got his date of six weeks.

Following our internal ITAR FPS meeting, we called for a two-week moratorium from the Customer for the project. Over those two weeks our team met to capture requirements from Josh's team, and finalized the requirements. Jim obtained a sign off on the requirements.

In another series of meetings, Tim, Jade, and I met with our customer Josh, where we discussed scope, and received a revised scope for the MVP delivery. Peter and I met with the customer's Enterprise Architecture (EA) group and got concessions on certain enterprise architecture requirements for the first MVP deliverable. We promised the EA group that we would follow the EA tenets, and our implementation would not prohibit implementation of future capabilities for the customer.

I discussed this with Peter and the team, and we decided to create a thorough data model first. With the data model done, the team leveraged an Object Relational Mapping (ORM) framework, and quickly stand stood up the Persistence layer and REST API. After that, the team spent many 12-hour workdays over six weeks. Tim took custom lunch orders every day for the team, while Jade provided coffee and desserts. With good teamwork after the initial failure, ITAR was able to deliver on schedule with a revised scope.

How It Impacted My Customer

Initially, my customer was excited that ITAR Corporation was going to deliver the project within the six-week timeline. Josh was unhappy when we informed him that the project schedule had to be revised, we had to change the scope of the Minimum Viable Product, and we wanted some concessions from the Enterprise Architecture group regarding enterprise architecture tenets compliance. Josh had informed the head of the new business unit that ITAR was going to deliver in six weeks so the timeline would not be revised, but the other changes were accepted. Josh understood what had happened and was willing to work with us to deliver a revised MVP in the six week timeline.

Josh had stressed that this was a very high visibility project for the company and the success of the project was critical for the new business unit. He helped our team get the concessions from the Enterprise Architecture group, and acted as a strong business sponsor. Josh had to explain the situation to the head of the new business unit and seek approval for the reduced scope, and this slightly affected his credibility as the plan had unexpectedly changed.

Overall, we all worked well as a team after the initial setback and were able to meet the customer timeline, but with reduced scope. The customer accepted the impact, and asked us to deliver more functionality in the next release. ITAR completed the project and went on to successfully deliver subsequent releases of the FPS software.

What Could I Have Done Differently?

I should not have accepted the situation we were placed in, and should have challenged the incorrect information shared by Jade. However, it was Jade who could have completely avoided the situation by doing things differently.

Immediately after winning the contract and putting together the team, Jade and Tim should have called an internal meeting of the FPS team and communicated the tentative draft of the project plan. Jade should have solicited inputs from entire team on level of efforts, milestone dates, time required in terms of duration, resource requirements, tools and license requirements, work breakdown structure sequencing, task/deliverable dependencies, critical path items and should have added in time for the MVP scope discussion. She should have then conducted a series of meetings with all customer stakeholders to solicit their requirements for security, compliance, enterprise architecture, operations, and infrastructure.

Jade should have incorporated all of the inputs into the project plan and should have had a review with ITAR FPS team to finalize the draft before reviewing with Josh, our customer, to get approval. This would have resulted in a project plan that was properly thought through and realistic in terms of scope and timeline.

What Did I Learn?

It is a good practice for people to follow established processes for delivering technology solutions, be it software, product, infrastructure, or applications. Complying with process can have a great positive outcome for the business and make architects more effective.

We can learn from other people's failures. Jade was the Project Manager from Hell. She made mistakes and misrepresentations, and put the team in an untenable position. To address this, I had to create a process that would work within the six-week timeframe. I made the necessary changes even though it burned the team out with 60-hour work-weeks for the duration of the project.

It is really simple… follow the process.

A Case of NICs on vSphere

This is a real-world example of an issue I worked on when I was a partner consultant for a leading IT outsourcing provider. In this case, the Network Interface Cards (NICs) were the culprit!

The Project

My customer wanted to upgrade the physical servers on their management stack while also upgrading to the latest VMware vSphere release. The existing servers were running vSphere 5.5, and they planned to upgrade them to vSphere 6.7.

Their network was already running 10Gb/s and was going to stay the way it was. Their vSphere management cluster consisted of four nodes, and had enough capacity to operate with only two nodes. We decided to migrate host-by-host because we had limited switch ports and rack space.

Everything was planned, and though we could easily have done the work without any downtime window, we scheduled a weekend to run the migration. All new hosts were validated during procurement against the VMware HCL (Hardware Compatibility List), and I confirmed that the latest firmware was deployed on hosts before the actual cutover.

It finally came time to start the migration. After arriving onsite, I was told that they had already replaced the first server, and had started to deploy VMware ESXi and VMware vCenter using their custom ISO images. After we had two of the new ESXi hosts operational we took down virtual machines on the old cluster, moved them, and restarted them on the new infrastructure. All validation processes went fine. We were done on time and the customer was happy.

The Failure

A few days later I got a call: "Something is wrong in the infrastructure...Backups are slower...We lose connections to management components"

We analyzed source issues but not much was visible. Everything looked good, except that data transfer rates were below 1 Mb/s instead of the 10Gb/s that we should have. We did not discover any issues on the physical NIC side of the host.

Next, we asked the networking team to check the switches for any errors. They confirmed that all links were up and marked 10Gb/s with no errors or faults, but throughput was low. This was weird! After further troubleshooting, we decided to validate whether it affected only certain hosts, so machines were moved around, but no...it affected all hosts. Given that we had other vSphere 6.7 clusters, we decided to migrate VMs to another cluster to see if that made any difference. As soon as machines were moved, all of the networking issues were resolved!

So, we had it narrowed down to the hosts. We ran down the HCL path again to see if we had missed anything, but the host was validated and listed as compatible via the HCL. Then, I asked for NIC information on the HCL. After the customer gave me the NIC information, I saw that it was non-compliant, so I asked them to go back to the vendor that sold them the hardware because the vendor had confirmed HCL compliance on the order. But, the vendor was not the problem as they had delivered the hosts without any NICs....

I then asked the customer why they had not validated the NICs against the HCL, and whether they had bought the NICs separately. They responded that they did not buy any new NICs. Where did the NICs come from? Someone had asked the vendor if the old server NICs might work in the new servers. Without validating the HCL, and without telling us, they had moved the NICs from the old to the new servers. Because the NICs worked with vSphere 5.5 no one had questioned whether they would work with vSphere 6.7. The root cause of the issue was related to the NIC drivers. As of vSphere 6.7, the old Linux-based drivers were no longer supported and vendors were not updating the older drivers with native drivers.

This failure had to be resolved through purchase, installation, and configuration of compatible NICs, resulting in additional delays in completing the project.

How This Impacted the Customer

The customer faced several days of problems. Fortunately, these problems existed only on the management cluster and did not affect any of their production workloads.

The troubleshooting process, research, and other activities affected multiple resources and took over 10 days. Considering that I was looking at only four hosts, this was quite some effort. The savings imagined from not replacing the NICs turned into a costly decision.

What Could I Have Done Differently?

There were several things that could have been done differently.

- Prerequisites: I should have reviewed the hardware configuration, which would have made it obvious that the NICs were not new, but were repurposed. I should have also made it clear to the customer that each component, not only the host, needs to be validated against the HCL.
- Validation: During the deployment, I should have done what I always preach to my students: do not believe what you are told without validation. Validate the configuration, driver, and firmware.
- Troubleshooting: From a troubleshooting perspective, we should have validated the HCL status of components again when the latest issue arose, but even more importantly, before initial deployment.

What Did I Learn?

This was an educational experience. I learned several things.

- Never trust that prerequisites are completed, and always re-validate them.
- Conduct evaluations (performance validation, baseline, and health check) before deployment into production.
- Perform a thorough evaluation of the hardware and software combinations using the HCL. The customer assumed that if the NICs worked with ESXi 5.5, then they would work with ESXi 6.7. Never assume!
- Simulate the upgrade manually or use a tool such as Runecast Analyzer to identify HCL compatibility issues like those within this story.

An upgrade simulation would have compared the current and proposed versions of hardware and software against the HCL, identifying the compatibility issue for the NICs. I/O devices are evaluated for the HCL on the basis of the combination of their drivers and firmware, so while we might not have been able to identify the driver if this was an OEM driver (and not found in the VMware HCL, as occasionally happens) for the target release, we would flag an issue if the firmware version were unsupported.

This experience demonstrates the need to validate assumptions, evaluate and confirm requirements, and cross-validate software and hardware changes with the HCL.

Know Your Audience

This is only one of the many stories that stayed with me over my 15+ years in the IT industry, but one that in hindsight, taught me so much.

The Project

It all started a of couple years ago with the request from a large international service provider who had struggled with their virtual machine deployment process. Their deployment of Linux and Microsoft Windows virtual machines took 1 to 1½ months to complete. The issue was not with the amount of time it took to deploy a virtual machine, but rather with the time it took to process all of the integrations such as backup, the Configuration Management Database (CMDB), monitoring, and so on. The customer required these integrations before a virtual machine could be taken over by the application teams to consume it.

The issue we saw with the different integration processes was that they all still relied on emails, telephone calls, and manual actions before a virtual machine could be added to the backup or CMDB. We could help. Most of the integration systems in question had an available API (Application Programming Interface) and we could improve the processes by leveraging automation.

After talking to the customer and collecting their requirements, we drafted the Statement of Work (SOW) that specified the project phases and deliverables. We branded the project "Project Zero-Touch" because we wanted to achieve fully automated delivery of a virtual machine without any manual intervention. We also selected two use cases, the deployment of Windows machines and of Linux machines. We estimated around six months to automate the full deployment process and complete the project.

After some back and forth about pricing, and more sales mumbo jumbo, the project was changed from a Time and Material (T&M) engagement to a fixed price project with a hard deadline. Everyone was happy that we could kick-off the project and get to work! Six months filled with long days of automation efforts followed. Every day we coded, validated, and optimized all different kinds of processes to streamline the deployment process.

The Failure

The most challenging factor was the customer's availability. We had to optimize all different kinds of processes from different teams within the customer's organization, and we had to rely on their teams' availability to describe their current process and work with us to optimize and automate the processes. Some teams could see the benefit of the project and were very cooperative, but other teams were reluctant to work with us because they thought we were there to automate their jobs away. (Yes, unfortunately this still happens.)

By the end of the project, the deployment time for the virtual machines and all their required integrations went from over one month to 25 minutes. Success!

We scheduled the project close meeting with the IT staff team, which was comprised of customer engineers, project leads, project managers, and the product owner. The goal for this project close meeting was to show the results and get final sign off for the project. It was a technical presentation where we showed what we had achieved, and we incorporated some demos about the automation workflow. At the end of the meeting everyone was positive and happy with the result, and they asked, "Can you also present this to the C-level executives"? We were excited to do so and to get sign-off on the project, so we enthusiastically replied that we could.

We gave the same presentation to the C-level executives. The presentation went smoothly, the demo was flawless and at the end of the meeting we asked if there were any questions. Everything went downhill from there, as the feedback was very negative.

> "Why are there only two catalog items available for deployment? We need to have more!"
>
> "Why is the deployment still taking 25 minutes?! We need to have it within 10 minutes!"
>
> "Why were six months needed for only this?"
>
> "We do not understand why we had to do this in the first place!"
>
> And finally: "We are not signing-off on the project as complete, because this is not meeting our expectations."

The C-level presentation was an utter failure. And the project had been changed from a T&M project to a fixed price project, so we did not have any time left. We needed time to go back to see if we could fix something without impacting our own project budget.

Where did we go wrong? Looking back at the meeting notes and questions we received it was clear. The C-level executives had not been correctly informed about the project, and what we presented was too technical and did not make sense to them. Fortunately, the fix was simple, and we asked for another session.

The second presentation was completely different from the first. We did not present anything technical; instead, we focused on the outcome of the project. We showed the financial benefit we had achieved, and provided show-back and some awesome pie charts with financial figures. It was a success! Because we were now talking on their level, they understood.

In the end the project got signed off as complete. We continued working on numerous other projects with the customer, but in a different, more agile form, and with a lot more communication between all levels.

How It Impacted My Customer

Because we had waited to present the result of the project until the last day before the deadline, we were unable to meet the deadline and it was marked as a "failed" project. People from the project team were demotivated because of it. Team members had put their heart into the project for the last six months and it had been marked as a failure. This can have a huge impact on the overall performance and attitude of people, and should never be taken lightly.

Also, the good relationship between us and the customer came under pressure. We had done exactly what was stated in the SOW and was agreed with all parties. But, this was not what the C-level executives were expecting, and you know what happens when an executive is unhappy.... People from both teams got dragged into different escalations meetings and were told that they had better fix it ASAP. Otherwise, it would cause a lot more stress in both organizations.

What Could I Have Done Differently?

- Set clear expectations: Yes, we had delivered all required items from the SOW, but the C-level executives were not impressed or happy. Avoid this as unhappy executives can make your life miserable.

  We should have asked for an Executive Sponsor to own the business case for the project. Then, at least one of the C-level executives would have been up to date on what had been agreed.

- Know your audience: Presenting an awesome technical solution where everything has been fully automated to a non-technical person is much like presenting a magic trick. The result looks simple but getting that result requires a lot of hard work and expertise! Be sure you are providing the correct level of the information to your audience.

If we had informed the different customer teams about why automation was important and beneficial during the kick-off for the project, there would have been less resistance from teams during the project. It is always better to avoid brute force and gracefully ease teams into automation.

What Did I Learn?

It is essential to set clear expectations and know your audience. Knowing your audience is everything, and is very often the difference between success and failure. We often see this in automation projects, as stakeholder buy-in outside of the core infrastructure team is typical.

A bit of research and preparation to customize reports and presentations to fit your audience can make or break your project. It is worth spending the time to make sure you are hitting the mark.

One topic I have not previously addressed is the *crawl, walk, run* approach. I would not advise anyone to approach an automation project where a fully deployed and integrated virtual machine is the only phase and deliverable. Instead, work in different phases. For example:

Phase 1: Deployment of virtual machine.

Phase 2: Integration A.

Phase 3: Integration B.

And so on....

After each phase check to see that all expectations are met and everyone is happy. A satisfied customer is the best source of advertisement, not only for your company but also for you personally!

Self-Absorbed Summer Camp Server

I got on stage holding a piece of paper with some handwritten notes in one hand...and a plunger in the other. Soon everyone on the room was laughing. Little did they know how terrified I was.

Wait, this story is supposed to be technical, right? Let me start again.

I got in the front of a classroom holding some notes in one hand...and a computer manual in the other. Soon everyone in the room was learning. Little did they know how terrified I was.

These two situations are related! How?

I favor this story with its lessons learned from summer camp over all those lessons about technical instruction, presentations, rapport building, and communication across a diverse audience, because of what it did for me personally. I have experienced failures in my technical career, but it was the lessons I learned from volunteering with kids at a summer camp, being put in charge of entertainment on stage, that helped me the most. Why?

Because architects *only* ever talk to a *single* stakeholder when creating and disseminating a solution, right? Architects *never* have to sit in a room full of people from different departments, roles, skills, and backgrounds to get them all to see and understand the technology *and* each person's other business needs, focus, agendas, and how it all fits together into a solution. An architect *never* has to work with diverse audiences and morph accordingly. And for a new architect, it is *never* scary conducting that first requirements gathering meeting, and with limited time and resources, creating and presenting a solution that everyone needs to understand.

Yes, that last paragraph is sarcastic. An architect has to be multi-faceted, not just with diverse technologies, but also with the many people wielding them. An architect needs technical skills and soft (people and communication) skills to communicate in ways that appeal to everyone, not just technical audiences.

To explore this, let us go to summer camp.

The Summer Camp Failure

I got on stage while holding a piece of paper with some hand written notes in one hand....and a plunger. Soon everyone on the room was laughing. Little did they know how terrified I was.

Later, a kid sat next to me in his wheelchair, and he knew the basics of juggling. A friend standing with me was an accomplished juggler and had taught me the basics of juggling, but it was not about him. We knew it was time to put the kid in the spotlight, show his skills, and make him the hero. Little did they know how terrified I was.

It was my first year at summer camp as a counselor, and I was totally out of my comfort zone. The camp was for children with neuromuscular disease. I was a noob (beginner) volunteering in this capacity, and was scared! Campers were kids from 6 to 21 years of age, and had different types of disability. Some walked with difficulty. Others had frail, thin frames, with dexterity but little strength. Many had assistive devices and/or were in large electric wheelchairs. Learning who they were as human beings and how to interact with them one-on-one, let alone in front of them on stage was, well...frightening.

I questioned myself as I started my job as camp counselor: Who was I to walk in and start interacting with these kids with my limited experience and lack of understanding of them and their needs? Would they see me as an outsider coming in to “fix” them, or as someone who insensitively projected what I had and what they did not? Or, perhaps, they would think that I was so keen to show my brilliance (despite my ignorance) while using them in my productions that I would somehow forget about them in the process? What did I really have to offer? Did I even belong there?

There was a need for entertainment, but few resources, and I was tasked with making something happen on the first day. In addition to pairing me with a camper, the director put me in front of everyone and said, "Make stuff happen. Here! Do skits!" He knew my skill set and, like a good manager who leads people according to their abilities, decided that despite my hesitation I was the one to put on stage as the new entertainment director. I had no clue. I was overwhelmed!

It was only for a week, but it was intense. Skit after skit failed miserably! It was insanely embarrassing when skits I thought were great fell completely flat with little to no laughter, and I was losing everyone's attention. So much for entertainment! But, I persisted and conjured up skits, jokes, and whatever else I could organize in short order, as difficult (and painful to my fragile ego) as it was.

A couple days into it I realized that I had stopped focusing on "people in wheelchairs" or "people with disabilities." Yeah, that reality existed, but I came to see all of the people in the room, myself included, as just kids with a need for laughter. I started to loosen up and focused less on how I came across, and more on how much they laughed. I listened to their stories, and then created skits and characters that were about them and their experiences at camp. I weaved everything together into themes that persisted throughout the week (and for years to come), so that the stories and laughs would keep coming back, and everyone had fun. Over the years, I added more juggling, props, skits, sounds, lights, stage direction, volunteers, and resources. Bigger and better for all of us!

Interestingly, my cycles of fear persisted and each year I again asked myself those same self-doubting questions. But, as before, within a day or two, the fear dissipated and I again saw all of us as a room full of kids. There was a need to be met, laughing, lots and lots of laughing, and my job was to facilitate that environment.

Technology Transfer and Presentation Failures

Jump forward a few years to the first technical class I taught as an instructor, and later to one of my first executive briefing center presentations while in a new role as a cloud architect. I initially thought that the time and effort I put into making summer camp succeed would detract from my work at as an engineer and instructor at the tiny virtualization company I worked for, but I was completely wrong.

The Technology Transfer Failure

I got in the front of a classroom holding some notes in one hand...and a computer manual in the other. Soon everyone in the room was learning. Little did they know how terrified I was.

Later a student asked a question, and another started to talk about what he thought was right. My mentors had taught me the basics. I knew that it was time to try to answer the student, and also to keep control of the classroom. I did not know the answer. It was time to put the spotlight on the guy who did. Make him the hero. But I did not.... Next slide.

The first class I taught as a noob instructor was for new virtualization software called VMware ESX. My co-instructor was not available, so it was up to me alone. I was out of my comfort zone and frightened as I taught students of different ages, experience, and technical backgrounds, all of whom, I thought, knew vastly more than I did.

Learning who they were as human beings and how to interact with them one-on-one, let alone being in front of all of them teaching a highly technical subject was, well...frightening.

I questioned myself as I started my first day as an instructor: Who was I to walk in and start interacting with these students, with my limited experience and lack of understanding of them and their needs. Who was I to teach a new class on software that I still did not quite entirely understand? Would they see me as an outsider coming in to "fix" them, or as someone who insensitively projected what I knew and what they did not? Or, perhaps, they thought I was so keen to show my brilliance that I forgot they were right in front of me as I persisted in my own bubble. What did I have to offer? Did I even belong there? Did they learn anything?

There was a need to educate, but few resources, and I was tasked with making *something* happen on my first day as a new instructor. In addition to creating class manual notes, I had to build the physical server kits used to teach classes for all of the instructors on our team, and then learn how to teach the class myself. The manager that had encouraged me to become an instructor saw me whiteboard for her, knew my skill set, and pushed me to teach. I felt like I had no clue. I was overwhelmed!

It was only for a week, but it was intense. I focused on the technology and keeping control. I thought it went well and then got the reviews. Mediocre at best.... My failure was self-absorption. I was so worried about knowing it all and keeping control that I failed to conduct the class in a way that was conducive to learning.

The Presentation Failure

Fast forward to my first executive presentation as a new cloud architect....

I walked into a briefing center full of executives, proud of my ability to present, and I started whiteboarding how a cloud is built, including many products from a large portfolio of software. Midway through the presentation, one the attendees interrupted me with a simple question that I attempted to answer. He then got agitated, so I tried to reexplain. Some others in the room also tried to help explain. I briefly put the spotlight on them, but quickly pulled it back to resume trying to explain again, controlling the room so I could get on with my presentation. If I said whatever I had to say enough times and just kept drawing on the white board he would get it. I was certain! But he got so frustrated that he was nearly yelling when he said,

> "You are saying vThis, and vThat, and v the other thing! And you are telling me about all these vThings! But I am not seeing how it all fits together! What are you talking about?!"

I was caught completely off guard. As I had presented many people were nodding their heads; people were getting it, I thought. I was on a roll until that moment. What was happening? This customer was getting more and more agitated and I could not explain my way out of it.

A few minutes later, one of our company executives walked in. I was in trouble. Without intending to, I had made a customer furious, and the executive was walking into a Hornet's nest that I had just stirred up. The executive looked at me and smiled as I stepped aside. He then asked the customer some key questions about what they were looking for. After getting some customer feedback, he explained to the customer how we were poised to meet their need with our suite of products natively integrated. The customer calmed down. The conversation took a 180-degree turn away from all the technology I had been spewing and towards customer pain points and solutions.

I had walked in the room with confidence based on previous success, and knew exactly what I was going to say. I walked out of the room feeling a major sense of embarrassment. What went wrong?

What was my failure? I was so self-absorbed and focused on what I was doing that I forgot to make it about them. I thought I had gotten over that! But here again, in a different situation, it took on a different flavor. This time I was overconfident. I was so focused on what I was going to say and show that I tried to force my presentation through. Our company executive saved the day. I had to again seriously evaluate how I conducted myself in presentations from classroom to briefing center (or anywhere) if I was going to call myself an architect.

How It Impacted My Customer

For the first several technical classes I focused most of my attention on talking through slides and trying to be technical. Students were exhausted by the end of the class and wanted to get out of there. They may have learned something, but I am not sure they got what they paid for. There is only so much anyone can learn at any one time without good mental breaks before they cannot absorb any more information. The rest becomes noise and bounces off of the student. A student goes from learning and relating technical concepts early on in a class to simply hearing technical words and thinking about dealing with it later.

For my presentation at the briefing center, my customer felt frustrated because I was talking at them instead of talking with them. I was minding my own business while I told the story I had prepared. They felt ignored and dismissed, and that frustration kept building until someone was able to engage with them on their level. Sadly, it was not me.

What Could I Have Done Differently?

In the technology transfer case, I just spewed forth slide after slide, despite knowing better. I should have listened to student needs, assessed their skills, encouraged information sharing, learned from them, and adjusted my presentation accordingly. I should have focused on telling why to use the technology, and not just on the features and what it does. One of the best pieces of advice I got from an instructor was this:

> You do not have to know all the technology. Focus on telling the story and let the students fill in the blanks. In telling the story, relate it to the impact of the technology to the end user, something they care about. Let the students learn through reading the slides, doing the labs, and interacting, not just you talking. Facilitate that interaction. Use analogies and metaphors and humor! Entertain! Lighten up the classroom from being purely technical work to technical work and play.

In the executive briefing, I should have arrived early (before my own presentation) to listen to and better understand the customer. Even with limited time for my presentation, I should have asked questions to show my willingness to listen, and to get a good heat map of customer need, skill sets in the room, and some of the personalities. I could then have tailored my presentation accordingly and created an environment to promote communication and learning, as opposed to just getting through my material.

What Did I Learn?

Overcoming my fear of looking bad on stage at camp helped me confidently teach students in a highly technical class after I realized my job was to facilitate the learning environment, including having fun. Performing on stage at summer camp opened up my communication skills as an instructor. Teaching and presenting complimented each other to help advance my career. I now teach and present (another word for teaching) to many different kinds of audiences, both technical and non-technical.

When presenting technical content it is only useful if it can be absorbed. Just as I can facilitate a skit on stage at summer camp without always being on stage, I can facilitate the classroom discussion without always doing the talking. Listen. Observe. Be aware. Take what students have said and done and repeat it. Share it again so that everyone benefits. Make it about them.

The following is a summary of what I learned:

- Make it about them. Period! People like to be heard, seen, and validated. A camper will become more interested, engaged and confident. A customer needs to know you are making it about them; otherwise, they may feel you have not really heard them and do not understand their needs.
- Fear is natural, but do not be so self-absorbed that you spend all your mental energy worrying about appearances or what you do or do not know. By the same token do not be so overly confident that you come across as being cocky. You will shift

in and out of your comfort zone. It is the nature of the job, especially when you are thrown into situations where you have to do everything.

- Gauge your audience and prepare appropriately. Be ready to morph your presentation from highly technical to novice-level, or from a technical to a business discussion, or even to call for separate meetings depending on the audience.
- Facilitate the learning environment by keeping it fresh and fun. Facilitate communication between all parties. Teach how to learn, not just what to learn.
- Make the people in the room the heroes. Leverage their knowledge to everyone's benefit. When someone speaks up, shine the spotlight on them and repeat what they said in a way that helps everyone understand, while giving credit to the original speaker.
- Do not be purely technical. Use analogies, stories, and metaphors to help build understanding and share ideas, but do not be afraid of being technical when you have to. Find the balance in every room, with every audience.
- As an architect it is our job to listen first, know our audience, and ask the right questions. We do not need to have all of the answers, but we must be able to relate solutions back to problems that our customers are trying to solve.
- Be willing to admit when you do not have the answer, but commit to getting one. Be willing to own your mistakes, and commit to correcting them. Be willing to fail, and learn from your failures.
- Do not project negativity. Absorb. Listen. Be a sponge. Gather requirements. Learn.

All of this takes practice....

Ransomware Recovery

This story is focused on a large organization. Like many companies, regardless of the industry, ITAR Corporation was undergoing the process of transforming itself to better compete with newer firms by delivering a new approach to age-old problems. ITAR made a commitment to modernize and refactor hundreds of legacy systems running in several Tier-1 datacenters. Over the past 24 months, several applications had been retired in favor of SaaS and others have started moving to the public cloud.

ITARs cloud-first strategy has undergone several iterations over the years and has cost the organization time, money and resources. One critical mistake ITAR made early on was to "lift-and-shift" several steady-state workloads to the public cloud. When they realized these workloads cost a tremendous amount of money to run "as-is" in a public cloud operating model, resources and budgets had to be reallocated to either refactor old apps or move them back on-premises. The original initiative to save money, while also providing a higher level of service to the business through migration to the public cloud, ended up becoming more of a resource drain in the short term. These starts and stops drained IT budgets causing ITAR's leadership to begin limiting IT funding to every division and cutting costs even in areas that were never part of the cloud migration initiative. This would prove to be shortsighted.

A division of ITAR, due to the unique nature of the business, had a siloed IT operation. It was under the corporate IT umbrella and shared the IT budget, but was not in-scope for any application refactoring or move to the public cloud. The infrastructure was simple, consisting of approximately 50 Remote Office/Branch Office (ROBO) sites, each with four servers and several workstations. These sites were linked to the corporate domain through a one-way trust. It was one of several divisions managed with a separate team of IT resources. This decentralized "edge" was an important and growing part of the business, primarily due to the steady increase of customers visiting those sites. Because the systems were relatively simple from an IT standpoint, the operational model that had been designed more than a decade ago still worked well. Although the footprint had nearly doubled in five years through acquisition and overall expansion, the process to bring up new sites and scale the operation was cumbersome, but manageable.

Like many ROBO operations, these sites lacked the innovation that is commonplace in the modern datacenter such as virtualization, shared storage, and high network throughput. IT leadership determined that a single server or even an entire site being down for a day was tolerable. Several years before, it had been determined that the cost to manually recover a single site was minimal compared to the cost of a full infrastructure overhaul in these locations.

The Project

Joan, the IT director responsible for the 50 ROBO locations had been creating a plan to bring several new facilities online in the upcoming calendar year, and this is where I got involved. The project was tied to an aggressive expansion of the business that involved three acquisitions, two greenfield sites, and the geographic consolidation of several other locations to more effectively cover the North American division. This would be the largest project Joan had undertaken since starting at ITAR six months previously, but we had successfully worked together in the past and she was confident.

The first facility was a new acquisition from an aging competitor in the space that could no longer effectively compete due to significant market consolidation. Although ITAR's other divisions had to reinvent themselves, this division was the market leader in its space.

Until now, all sites under this business unit had been considered equal from an IT perspective regardless of their size. Each would require the deployment of a "cookie cutter" build consisting of physical servers, networking gear, the rack, power, and cooling to house the infrastructure. After the gear arrived, Joan's team followed a standard procedure to get everything online. The process was a standard "rack and stack" and the tedious task of manually installing operating systems on each server, followed by the installation and configuration of each application. The build consisted of approximately 230 manual steps. Although the site was considered standard, it would still require weeks of planning and 1-2 weeks of work to get it online. Joan and I had been working with her team to identify a better way to deploy and manage these sites. From previous experience, we both knew that the current method of deployment amounted to "keeping the lights on" and would not be sustainable forever.

The Failure

It was about 4:00 p.m. and Joan and I had just wrapped up a status call with her team when she received a call from one of ITAR's midsize facility managers informing her that the web application used to process data from the plant's equipment could not be accessed. This was not uncommon as the team received an alert like this about once a week. Although critical to the overall function of the operation, the site's equipment would continue to operate for at least 48 hours. Order processing and billing would be slightly delayed, but it usually took only a simple service restart or a reboot to get the process running again. Joan assured the facility manager that everything would be operational within the hour.

Joan was about to connect to VPN to run the standard restart script when she received a call from a manager at one of the other locations reporting a similar issue. While she was on the phone, John, an engineer on her staff, sent her a text indicating he had also received a call and was not able to connect to the site remotely to address the issue.

It was clear that something was wrong. Because the individual sites had no dependence on each other, she wondered if it could have been the result of a major ISP outage, but quickly ruled that out as each site had redundant ISP connections into their Multiprotocol Label Switching (MPLS) cloud. Then, Joan received a call from Maggie, ITAR's VP of Corporate Infrastructure.

Maggie informed Joan that the organization had been compromised by what appeared to be a ransomware attack, and many Windows-based data drives had been encrypted by the attacker. The impact was still being evaluated, but Joan was instructed to steer clear of any network resources for now and not login via VPN. Triage began immediately as Joan contacted her staff and notified each location's facility manager. John then texted her indicating his laptop had also become inoperable, and all he could access was a Notepad document on his desktop. When he opened the document, there was an ominous message in broken English stating his laptop had been encrypted.

Joan suspected that her division had been hit hard by the hackers. Based on a series of frantic phone calls and text messages, she braced herself for what was to come next. At her former employer, Joan managed an environment that was that was 90% virtualized. There were trainings and business continuity plans, but she had not seen any such plans in place here. There was so much work to do to get new sites on-line and keep the operation moving that planning for a disaster was at the bottom of the list. She did not immediately grasp the impact, but the harsh reality started to sink in that the environment was built entirely on stand-alone physical servers. Not having snapshots, a centralized management solution, or the ability to do data recovery from tape for each location would make recovery a nightmare scenario. Additionally, only basic remote operations were possible due to the abysmally slow 10 Mb/Sec WAN connection.

A Costly Recovery Effort

ITAR had defined a 48-hour Recovery Time Objective (RTO) for each of the remote sites. This was the acceptable amount of time for systems to be down before there would be a revenue impact. The 48-hour RTO was achievable for the full recovery of a single site, but recovering 50 sites with three people on staff was impossible.

Joan's team and I spent the next day assessing the impact and consolidating the manual recovery documents they had created during each site's initial deployment, as well as planning the logistics of the recovery. Because the attackers had used an enterprise administrator account to gain control of all Active Directory connected devices, every Windows-based device that touched the corporate domain was compromised and would have to be rebuilt.

For the ROBO operation, there was no easy way to get the business back online, and all machines would need to be manually rebuilt. Although the plan Joan had been working on prior to being notified of the outage included adding some level of HA through virtualization and enhanced network speeds with SD-WAN, due to timing and approvals, none of this could be incorporated into the recovery effort.

The rebuild operation for each site would consist of the installation and configuration of four servers (SQL, AD, file server, and a web server) and up to six application workstations. There were 200 servers and approximately 200 workstations in all. Sites were split up between Joan and each member of her team. ITAR also provided two consultants for each location to assist in the process.

The scope of the outage went far beyond what was initially found. The ransomware attack was a catastrophic event for all divisions including the corporate datacenters where, at least, there were mechanisms in place to allow for faster remediation. Hypervisors, Linux-based storage systems, and public cloud instances were not affected. The Windows guests were affected but could be more easily recovered by restoring snapshots. A setback for the corporate team was that one day into the recovery forensic analysis indicated the malicious code had been introduced one month prior. Snapshots that were recovered had to be patched and application data had to be fully scanned before any restores were performed. They were still able to meet most of the Recovery Time Objectives, including RTOs defined in their Business Continuity plans.

Approximately 30 hours after first being notified, Joan and her team had a plan and began the process of recovery in their local facility. Travel schedules and recovery deadlines for each ROBO site were defined and the team acclimated to the idea that there would be significant time away from their families for up to three weeks.

In the days following the attack, corporate leadership realized that recovery of the ROBO operation, one of ITAR's most important divisions, was a monumental effort that would still require weeks of recovery time. Although six sites had come back on-line in just two days, there were still 44 to go and they were starting to miss internal SLAs. It was clear that revenue would be impacted. Executive management even considered the idea of paying the hijackers the ransom they were demanding to unlock their systems. The sound advice of corporate lawyers insisted that ITAR not pay off a criminal organization. How can you trust them to adhere to their guarantees of paying the ransom?

Fifteen days after the initial call, Joan and her staff had successfully brought all 50 sites back on-line ahead of schedule—a truly heroic effort! During the recovery effort, sites were prioritized and processes were shifted to different locations, but there was a still a significant revenue impact to the business. Although management was relieved that they had survived the attack and recovery times were shorter than anticipated, they questioned what could have been done not only to prevent the attack, but what technologies could help them if as similar event happened again in the future. Joan and her team had some ideas….

What Could I Have Done Differently?

There was not a lot of opportunity to do things differently in this case, but things could be done better going forward. Datacenter modernization is top of mind for most IT organizations. Although it can be logical to prioritize the corporate datacenters, ROBO sites should also be a focus for modernization.

The ROBO team at ITAR focused on the following specific areas to modernize their operation:

- Mitigation: What steps could be taken to prevent such an attack in the future?
- Resiliency: What could be done to make the ROBO sites more resilient, preventing outages that could be the result of a variety of circumstances (security event, natural disaster, extended power outage, and so on)?
- Recoverability: How could ROBO locations be brought quickly back on-line and achieve an acceptable RTO with a limited staff?

Although a robust security framework is the most important step in preventing or at least mitigating an attack, the ransomware hackers gained access through a corporate system account that propagated through Active Directory. There was little the ROBO team at ITAR could do to protect themselves in this case. Of course, they reviewed all processes and every measure would be taken to make sure that branch staff were properly trained, and that systems were properly secured.

ITAR determined that tackling the resiliency and recoverability problem at all locations would be the immediate priority, and after this event was “magically” able to get funding from the business. Joan expanded on her plan to not only include new sites that would be deployed this year, but also apply ROBO modernization practices to all sites.

Further research and investigation showed that much of the technology found in today’s modern datacenter that inherently solves for resiliency and recoverability can also be applied to small branch locations with a price point that is far more reasonable than in the past. This is a result of software-defined architectures such as Hyperconvergence, which reduce form factor and can be scaled to accommodate either very small or very large environments.

In summary, we can all learn from the pain felt after ITAR suffered through a ransomware attack. Any system, regardless of location can be susceptible to such an attack. Most organizations still prioritize branch locations differently than corporate datacenters, sometimes disregarding the business impact of a major outage.

In the past, hardware and software designed to provide fault tolerance and resiliency were not financially attainable for small ROBO sites and manual recovery was the only option. Fortunately, solutions can now be deployed that provide the highest levels of security, resiliency and recoverability in a very small form factor. Hopefully sharing these lessons from a very real series of events can prevent history from repeating itself in your IT operation.

What Did I Learn?

Although the ransomware attack affected ITAR's entire corporate network, the remote offices were particularly vulnerable, as illustrated by ITAR's experience. Now that the dust has settled, ITAR is rethinking how branch offices should be deployed, protected and managed. There are many lessons to be learned, many of which are obvious when reading through the narrative.

Consider how some of the following high-level lessons learned by ITAR may apply to your organization:

- Remote Offices usually provide a critical function to the business and in most cases should be given the same operational priority as the core datacenter. Although ROBO sites do not share the complexities that core datacenters have, do not assume they are not important. If I had helped Joan and ITAR realize this earlier, this situation could have been avoided or, at least, the impact minimized.

- Downtime can be incredibly expensive, and organizations should invest to protect themselves from worst-case scenarios in all IT silos. I did not lead ITAR far enough down this path as we never considered *all* remote sites *and* corporate going down at the same time. I now have much more respect for Murphy's Law.

- ROBO site outages are not always isolated. Ransomware attacks, virus outbreaks, and even application rollouts can bring multiple sites down at one time.

If staff is limited, investments in automation should be made to streamline deployment and recoverability of critical applications. The highly repeatable processes of building, maintaining, and recovering critical ROBO environments are a perfect use case for automation.

Depending on the application, delivering high availability and resiliency can be expensive. IT leadership should outline realistic downtime scenarios to the business and let them decide what an acceptable Recovery Time Objective should be. While I did work with Joan to get an Recovery Point Objective (RPO) and Recovery Time Objective (RTO) defined for each site, we missed the larger disaster scenario where those RPO/RTO numbers could not be achieved. Again...no one thought that *all* sites would go down!

The post-incident forensic analysis revealed that the ransomware attack that affected ITAR likely started with an internal employee opening a malicious email. Although there are innumerable security solutions to mitigate such malware from propagating across an entire organization's network, new vulnerabilities crop up daily. Learning how to better educate the team's security awareness, implementing the right tools, defining and adhering to an enforced security standard, and providing and auditing regular training to employees is critical for all organizations. ITAR rated themselves as a B+ across all these areas, but perhaps their rating failed to take some risks into account as the attackers still found a way in.

One Redundant Desktop

This story looks at things from the sales engineer perspective. I cried over this project while it was underway!

A while ago I was helping a sales team architect a VDI (Virtual Desktop Infrastructure) solution for an organization. They were looking to deploy VDI to all of their users, from the CEO to the janitors, and everyone in between. Additionally, they wanted a self-service portal to request desktops, making them easy to consume and manage.

The Failure

This was a straightforward ask, though things got more complex as we talked with the customer. They wanted to implement this as an active/active VDI solution. In other words, they had several sites where the VDI solution would be deployed, and users could get a desktop from the "nearest" site.

It became even more complex as we explored the types of users they had. They had the typical users you would expect: secretaries, executives, office workers, and so on. All of these users were fairly straightforward use cases for VDI, even in an active/active multi-site design, but they also had an engineering group.

The engineers needed powerful GPUs (Graphics Processing Units) to do their work. Additionally, according to the IT team, these users rarely logged off their laptops and saving their work could take more than 30 minutes. They would lock their laptops and leave for lunch or go home and let the system render (run a workload on a GPU) whatever they were working on.

We had a dedicated meeting with the engineering users. We wanted to know as much as we could about them. Our biggest question was about the active/active site configuration and what their expectation was for their desktops. We were told that the engineers needed to be part of the active/active solution, that the desktop configuration had to be identical down to the location of the icons, that applications they had open had to be restored, and the content in the applications must be maintained. A crash-consistent state was not acceptable. (*Crash consistent* means that the desktop would be in a state as if you pulled the plug on a computer and any work that had not been saved would be lost.)

This surprised our team. We investigated the options that could be used to meet all of these requirements and came up with answers for how to accomplish all but one. We did not have a way to deliver VDI for an active/active site that was better than crash consistent with GPUs. This meant that any work an engineer had not saved would be lost, and they would have to redo that work.

During our next meeting with the customer, we wanted to rationalize the constraint of desktops needing to be more than crash consistent. It was not physically possible to have virtual desktops span two or more active sites and be anything better than crash consistent.

To rationalize the conflicting constraints, we met with the customer and presented a list of questions that should help us identify some alternatives.

- Do the engineers roam from site to site?
- What is the impact today if an engineer's desktop crashes?
- Would crash-consistent engineering desktops be better than the physical desktops they currently have?
- Is there a scenario where all of the engineers at a given site could lose their desktops? If so, what is the organizational impact?

The customer's stakeholders and some engineering users at this meeting helped us and we discovered the following:

- Engineers do roam from site to site, but they were worried that engineers at Site A when running a virtual desktop from Site B, would have a worse user experience than an engineer who was at Site A running their desktop from Site A.

- Currently, when an engineering user's laptop crashed the engineer would lose their work and it would take a day or two to get a replacement laptop. Plus, the engineer had to redo all of the work that was lost. This could have a seven-figure impact.
- A crash-consistent desktop may have some advantages, such as allowing an engineer quicker access back to their work, but it also has a bigger impact if things go wrong. If a server crashed and there were 12 engineers working on it all of them may need to redo a day's worth of work. The impact could be in excess of 8 figures to the organization. While exploring the impact of a full site disaster it was discovered that something impacting half of the engineering team could destroy the organization.
- The only scenario where a site could be disrupted would be a catastrophic building failure, which was much less likely than a row of servers failing.

We took these responses back to see if there was some way to rationalize the constraints and deliver an active/active VDI environment that provided something better than crash consistency for the engineering desktops.

In the end, we could not find a way to support the request. Ultimately the only way to deliver the desired user experience would be to create a stretched cluster between two or more sites, with engineering desktops that leverage a VMware Fault Tolerant configuration that would have duplicate VMs running in lock step using GPU technology. This, of course, was not possible. Even if it had been possible, the bandwidth required to achieve it between two sites would be immense.

We explained the limitations of the technology and diagramed it out for the customer. We even suggested user training and behavior modification to reinforce saving changes and logging off when done. With the constraints explained we let the customer choose.

The customer chose to continue to use high-end laptops for their engineers. They concluded that because it was impossible to achieve anything more than crash-consistent virtual desktops, the potential financial impact to the organization was too great.

We were able to implement a VDI environment for many of their non-engineering users.

How It Impacted My Customer

Because we could not build an active/active site that was more than crash consistent for the customer, the engineers continued to use high-end laptops to complete their work.

This also meant that the VDI environment needed to be scaled back, because part of the funding for the VDI initiative was allocated for the engineering team. Without the expected budget, some features such as a self-service portal were cost prohibitive.

This changed the infrastructure design. Because of the limited number of engineer desktops that could fit on a single ESXi host, the environment would have required many racks of servers. Without these engineering desktops, the smaller VDI project consumed less space in their datacenters.

There were several engineers (and many on the IT team) who were excited about not having to carry laptops, and looked forward to all the features they would have had access to with VDI. Unfortunately, they did not get to take advantage of the features that VMware Horizon offered.

This also posed an ongoing set of security considerations for them. Because the engineers still use physical laptops there is a potential risk that the laptops could become lost and the engineering data on them compromised. It was not possible for us to calculate the cost to the business if that data were to be compromised.

What Could I Have Done Differently?

I said that I had cried over this project. I did! I had been on a few calls with the customer, and I had the whiteboard in my office filled with preliminary numbers for the architecture and had massive Excel spreadsheets calculating user densities for different scenarios. A team member kept rounding my numbers. This changed the performance requirements of the environment by about 10%. I asked the team member to stop rounding the numbers but he did not, and the situation continued to escalate. This person finally called my boss to complain that I was not allowing numbers to be rounded, and things were resolved in favor of presenting accurate (unrounded) information to the customer.

Later, I was onsite for a customer visit. We were halfway into a meeting and were clarifying our understanding of their environment. I got up and started whiteboarding the requirements they were giving us. I wrote the unrounded numbers I had prepared earlier on the board, and was able to calculate several aspects of useable capacity for the customer. The customer instantly understood this. My rounding co-worker, I think, also finally understood why the 10% difference was important. Since then we have gotten along and worked well together.

From this experience I learned a lot about perseverance and not allowing myself to be bullied. It is important that those of us with a technical understanding not allow the solution to be minimalized only to look good on paper or sound good in a sales pitch. This is one of the most valuable lessons I learned from this engagement.

Working with the customer on the acceptance criteria turned out to be another important thing I learned from my time with them. A typical approach might be to ask, “if it does all of these things, is it acceptable?” Instead, we asked the customer to work jointly with us to define the success criteria. As a result, we got much better buy-in from the customer, discovered that some of what we thought was important was not, and identified things we needed to include in further acceptance testing.

More Analysis

Earlier I mentioned the impact a host or system failure would have on the organization and how catastrophic it could be. In my role on this project I should have taken the time to do the actual calculation of mean time between failures (MBTF) for the hardware, the likelihood of unplanned outages with the software, and many of the other factors that tie into the failure scenario.

I could have also contrasted those calculations with the probabilities of the way things were at the time and the exposure to the organization; for example, accidently spilling coffee on or dropping a laptop. That does not include the security exposure with physical systems, be they removable storage devices or root kits.

Had I performed an analysis with details and cost figures, I could have taken it to the customer and had a meaningful conversation about the risks. It might have been the pushback needed to keep the engineering desktops in scope for the project.

Something I Did Wrong as an Architect

I was not able to get the customer to purchase what we wanted to sell them because my initially proposed solution did not fit their needs. The architecture process should *never* be about what you want to sell. It should always be about helping the customer reach their goals.

A lot of people were watching this project and there were high expectations for the solution. I had serious conversations with a few people about business outcomes and product positioning. I am sure if you were to ask them, I failed to position the product.

Furthermore, we had to stop positioning one of the main products we had intended to use in the offering because of issues that would prevent us from satisfying the customer's needs. Many were displeased by my recommendation to remove it from scope, but after discussing it with my management it was determined that removing it was best for the customer.

What Did I Learn?

From this experience the customer, team, and I learned a lot about what is possible with GPUs. We improved our ability at analyzing constraints and explored whether it was possible to expand reality. We also helped each other become better VDI architects.

This was the first time I worked with a customer who had significant security requirements that were part of day-to-day operations. Security made it very difficult to determine the sizing for virtual desktops as I was not allowed to observe or even collect usage statistics. From this I learned to be creative when asking questions about how the desktops were used. I used my past experience to approximate what the users were doing on their desktops. By doing this we were able to help the customer build a small testing environment to test assumptions and get user feedback about the experience. Though not my first time building and using a test environment, it was the first time I could not have direct access to the results or the environment.

From this I discovered the power of having a well-defined test plan and acceptance criteria. We first trained the customer how to build the test VDI environment, and then we worked with the customer to define what a passing criterion was for user experience.

The customer learned a lot about VDI and leveraging GPU virtualization. Though they did not deploy virtual desktops with vGPUs in their environment for their engineering team, they leveraged much of what they learned to deliver their next IT project, and looked to us as trusted advisors in their VDI journey.

The last thing I learned is how happy I am that I wrote all of this down. It has been a while since I looked at this project folder and it is immense. I have hundreds of emails, notes, and architectural designs for this project. As I go back and review them to refresh my memory I cannot believe how influential this project was in my career, the things I learned, and the people I met. So, as a final tip, take time to write up your experiences, and review them later to see how you have grown.

A Bad Assumption and Neglected Diligence

This was my first big VDI project, sold by a third party to a big government organization. The third-party company could not deliver the scope of work, so I was contracted as a senior consultant to design and deploy the project.

The Project

The project consisted of a 1200-user VDI environment. It needed to run in two datacenters because of a 99.9% availability requirement. This drove the calculations for both affordable loss (Recovery Point Objective, or RPO) and unplanned downtime (Recovery Time Objective, or RTO). Based on this, there was a requirement for a 4-hour RPO, and a 1-hour RTO.

The customer had an older version of VMware View running that was not capable of spreading across two datacenters. They had also virtualized most of their in-house applications into VMware ThinApp packages. The apps varied in size between 500 MB and 2.5 GB. The customer had encountered some serious logon and application starting time issues.

I had worked with the Dynamic Environment Manager (DEM) and previous versions with different product names for many years. I had also worked with App Volumes (previously named Cloud Volumes). The signed Statement of Work did *not* include DEM and App Volumes solutions to be added to the VDI stack. The suggested solution from the third-party company was to add all of the applications to the base image and use persona management[4] to replace their roaming profiles.

4 Persona Management in the context of VMware VDI, is a feature that stores and delivers user-specific data to virtual or physical desktops. The data is pulled from a remote storage repository.

I had some great discussions with the customer's IT teams during the first week of the project. I identified their issues, main goals, and drivers. I also got to know the customer's culture. The hardware stack consisted of Vblocks and XtremIO, solutions that have been used in many VDI solutions and are proven to deliver performance at scale. After finishing the conceptual design, which was signed off by the customer, it was time for the logical design, and time to choose the solutions to use in the VDI stack.

Although the third-party company had sold the customer on using persona management and ThinApps in the base image, I thought there was a better solution for the customer's issues. I communicated the value of the recent VMware acquisitions in the EUC space by showing how they could avoid issues that were commonly seen with the technology they had in place.

The long application starting times were a different issue. App Volumes could deliver ThinApps to a virtual desktop, and I was convinced that this was the perfect solution for the customer issues. And as App Volumes was already available from the customer's My VMware account, it was enterprise ready as well, right? (No...I was wrong!)

IT engineers and architects sometimes tend to over-engineer when it is not required, unnecessarily placing themselves in a bad position when something goes wrong.

The third-party company racked and stacked the hardware, and after testing I installed the Horizon stack with VMware User Environment Manager (UEM) and App Volumes. Everything went well with the first group of users. We had a small group of ThinApps inside a single AppStack and UEM profiles linked to the apps. As I expected, logon times and application starting times were reduced to a minimum and the user experience was good. Logon only took about 10 seconds, and applications started within a second. The whole team was happy because we had delivered beyond expectations. We had 50 users in production before the first deadline, so we were excited!

The entire migration was not in scope for our assignment. We were only responsible for the first groups of users (including the applications), and the customer's IT team ran the rest of the migration. After our part was finished, the customer had 150 users in production and was still very satisfied. We thought we had finished the project with a happy customer.

The Failure

After a couple of weeks I got a call from the third-party company. The customer had serious logon issues. They had migrated around 200 ThinApps to AppStack and had about 800 users on the platform in production. As they had increased the number of users and apps, the logon times had increased as well. The solution did not scale well.

App Volumes at that time had some serious caveats:

- The App Volumes filter driver slowed down the logon process with every AppStack that was attached.
- The earlier versions were not able to attach AppStacks synchronously, so App Volumes Managers were able to handle only a couple of attachments per second.
- The configuration maximums were not fully documented.
- In terms of sizing the environment, no one really knew how many attach operations a single App Volumes Manager could handle.

When they escalated the issue the logon time typically exceeded one minute, and two minutes was not an exception. The customer had submitted multiple tickets to support, but support was not able to solve the issues. All Hell broke loose!

Ultimately, we had to revert to using ThinApps, some streamed from the network and others deployed in the base image, to decrease the logon time again.

How It Impacted My Customer

Several of my choices impacted the customer.

- The design changes resulted in poor logon performance that impacted the customer's productivity and acceptance of the new system.
- The customer was impacted by the additional time it took to finalize the project and remove all issues, though they were not charged for the corrective actions.

The third-party company had not expected issues because of their trust in me.

What Could I Have Done Differently?

Bad assumptions can cause your solution to fail or function less than optimally. You need to understand the impact, define risks, and mitigate them with effective design decisions. In this case I incorrectly assumed that App Volumes would scale without issues, causing serious delays when logging in. I early-adopted a technology into a project without first consulting the software vendor. It would have saved me from a lot of issues if I had. I neglected to do due diligence.

Architects need to be creative. If we just followed reference architectures, there would be no need for architects. However, reference architectures and best practices do not fit every environment or situation, and architects need to be creative to satisfy customer requirements. Keep in mind that a SOW is a legally binding contract and may limit how creative you can be while aligning with the project goals and the SOW. I should have followed the SOW, or undergone a formal process to have it updated when the original design was changed.

What Did I Learn?

My creativity, opportunism, and some bad assumptions led me into this failure. I used my soft (communication and people) skills to sell a solution like a salesperson, but I failed to think like an architect and fully evaluate the risks. You must perform due diligence to identify all risks and prepare a plan to mitigate them before implementing your solution, and you must deliver the work product defined in the SOW.

This project led me to realize that I had to take my architecting skills to a next level.

My VCDX Journey

A colleague had just started his VMware VCDX journey, which inspired me to do the same. I felt like the world's worst architect, and I needed to grow!

I started my VCDX journey in 2015, and finished in October 2016 after a successful first attempt. I learned more than I could have imagined. It is a cliché, but entirely true: the journey is as important as the destination. I learned to think like a VCDX. I will never, ever, get into a situation like the one in this story again!

Becoming a VCDX changed me. It improved my skills and gave me the confidence to work on any project as an architect. Independent of the size or complexity, the VCDX methodology helps me to successfully deliver a design that can be implemented with the lowest possible amount of risks. I did not have the necessary skills for this project. Knowing what I know now, I would apply the VCDX methodology for success.

Support Matters

In 2012, I was working for a bank in a major city. It was a young bank with an IT infrastructure that had been built seven years previously using a turnkey bare-metal solution from one vendor with a mix of x86 and non-x86 hardware. Over three-years we had virtualized 95% of the workloads to VMware vSphere including the migration of software running on Unix to x86 with Linux. Only the Core Banking system and ATM Switch were still running on non-x86 hardware.

During the consolidation process we had effectively exhausted our storage capacity so we completed the Request for Proposal (RFP) process for purchasing a new storage solution. We selected two storage vendors from the vendor short-list; one was the incumbent vendor we worked with to build the original solution, and the other was a leading global storage vendor. We had been decommissioning all of the incumbent vendor's software products due to expensive software licensing, poor vendor support, and unnecessarily complex software products.

The main requirement of the RFP was to have a storage replication technology that would support the Core Banking system. We had a legal requirement from the Central Bank to be disaster tolerant for that function. We had tried using the Core Banking system's native database replication technology, but it repeatedly failed after a few days of replication consistency and the software vendor never provided a resolution.

The technology team was in favor of selecting the leading storage vendor as the replacement, but the incumbent vendor did a deal with the bank's COO by significantly lowering the price to undercut the competition. The technology team was told about the decision after the fact and when we complained, we were instructed to begin the project implementation.

The Project

Three months after the RFP decision, we had implemented the majority of the storage upgrade project and most systems had been migrated to the greenfield storage solution.

The application owners were very happy with the performance of the new solution and the only remaining task was storage replication to the DR site for the Core Banking application, which despite multiple trials, did not work when tested. The storage replication issue turned into an extended task that was still incomplete after the storage transition was completed and the legacy storage platform had been decommissioned.

The storage vendor worked with our Unix Administrator, who along with me became a de-facto owner of the new storage solution. The brownfield storage solution had been maintained by the datacenter manager who did not have time to learn the new technology, which consisted of All-Flash and 15K Fiber Channel drives and a storage virtualization layer for federating multiple storage arrays. The storage vendor kept us on a storage upgrade journey that they claimed would solve the replication issue.

We had an approved, perpetually open change request and the Unix Administrator was under strict instructions from the CIO to get storage replication working because our annual audit with the Central Bank was coming soon.

The Failure

One weekend, nine-months after the storage migration project had completed, the Unix Administrator was again upgrading the storage virtualization layer when he called and told me that the storage at the primary site was behaving strangely after the upgrade. The datacenter operators also noticed extremely poor performance and some of the smaller systems were crashing.

He asked me what he should do. I asked him to open a new ticket with the storage vendor with the highest level of criticality and let them follow their process. I also called my colleague (we both reported to the CIO as his joint CTOs), and explained the situation.

An hour later I called the Unix Administrator for an update and he told me that vendor support was still validating our support contract number and would not provide support until that process had been completed. Our storage vendor did not have a direct line to call for second- or third-level level support and get immediate assistance for critical issues. Everything had to be done through a clunky web UI.

I called the CIO and apprised him of the situation. We were concerned that the business-critical applications would crash and decided that the best course of action was to gracefully shut down all systems at the primary site (it was still the weekend), work with vendor support to get the storage issue resolved, and get back online before 9:00 a.m. the next day. The CIO agreed and also called our local partner to assist. We were very sensitive to the Core Banking system crashing because the consistency of the crashed database required months of manual database record restores from backups.

At 4:00 p.m. that afternoon, I drove to the bank's primary datacenter to take care of what I mistakenly thought was going to be a fairly simple task. It started quite easily. I asked the datacenter operators to start their shutdown tasks. They were very experienced at bringing the systems online and offline and followed documented procedures.

Things got difficult with the support call to the storage vendor. By 9:00 p.m. we still did not have a vendor expert on the line to assist us. The CIO had arrived on-site and was so frustrated he decided that we should try to resolve the issue ourselves by performing power resets of the storage sub-systems. I argued against this, but he was the boss so we pulled power plugs on the storage equipment, all to no avail. Things got worse…eight storage virtualization nodes were hanging on the BIOS boot screen.

By 9:00 a.m. the next morning we still did not have vendor support and the bank staff was coming into work. Some staff decided to visit the datacenter to see what the fuss was all about. At one point we had 50 people standing around chatting in the datacenter. This was a distraction—it was not helpful to have non-essential personnel in a crisis area.

At 10:00 a.m., our local partner engineer finally got a vendor expert on the vendor's partner remote chat platform to start providing support. The vendor expert refused to join a conference call with me or use collaboration software to communicate more easily. Because our web proxy was offline we could not get Internet access, so we had to use the CIO's personal 3G access point to connect to the Internet. I had to use Yahoo Messenger with the local partner engineer to collaborate and share files, which he cut and paste to the vendor's remote chat session (which, as a customer, I did not have access to). My laptop also had a LAN connection to the datacenter network to access the storage management interface.

At 4:00 p.m. that afternoon, after a downgrade of the storage platform and many file copies to rebuild the storage virtualization metadata across all nodes, the storage solution was back online. It took the datacenter operators another two hours to bring every system back online, and then the application owners had to perform consistency checks to ensure no data had been lost. By 9:00 a.m. the following workday, everything was back to business as usual.

The root cause of the issue was the version of the storage software provided to the Unix Administrator. The software was still being tested and was not generally available (GA) yet. The vendor should not have shared that version with the bank. We also had people and process gaps that allowed this situation to occur.

How It Impacted My Customer

We were down for more than 24-hours and we failed our Central Bank audit because we did not have DR functioning for the Core Banking application.

The CIO also had political issues with the bank's C-Level executives as this outage was very embarrassing and could have been avoided. This led to him being fired a year later.

What Could I Have Done Differently?

There are several things I could have done differently.

- Business Value: I clearly remember a meeting with the CIO and COO where they asked for my opinion about the RFP short list and how to proceed. In particular, they asked about the difference between the two storage vendors and which was best for the bank. I talked about the technology value which, in hindsight, did not register with them. I should have described the business value, where terms such as maintaining SLAs, brand protection, and maintaining Central Bank audit compliance would have been more readily understood than my confusing technical jargon.
- Change Management: Having a perpetually open approved change request for a critical infrastructure component such as the storage solution was a bad idea. We should have reviewed every new action plan the storage vendor proposed and assessed the risk before executing it.
- Storage Skills: We should have included a vendor-resident engineer in the Storage RFP to own and operate the new storage solution. Having an infrastructure platform without dedicated, skilled engineers to own and manage the different sub-systems poses a risk that could impact your customers. If you cannot hire people with the skills, look into using vendor-provided resident engineers or outsourcing to a Managed Service Provider (MSP).

- Know Your Applications: The inherent problem with the Core Banking system database was its architecture. It was essentially a flat file system with open files that were being replicated at the block level. We could not achieve database consistency at the DR site during testing. It worked during switchover with a graceful shutdown of the application (the consistent state was replicated), but during failover the crash-consistent copy of the database had thousands of open files that were never closed and required months of manual rework to fix. Using storage replication for disaster recovery of this particular database was never going to work. We should have switched to a modern Relational Database Management System that supported multi-site replication to solve the Core Banking system disaster recovery function.

The Aftermath

The outage had a lasting impact.

- One Month Later: The incumbent storage vendor was terminated and told never to visit our offices again.
- Three Months Later: We transitioned the storage platform to a solution from the leading global storage vendor. It cost the bank a significant amount of time and money to fix the mistake, but the new platform worked well. That experience set the tone for all of our vendor support relationships and we always paid for business-critical support moving forward.
- Two Years Later: We successfully refactored the Core Banking system to run on VMware vSphere with a modern operating system and a modern database that used native database replication to the remote site.

What Did I Learn?

There were several key takeaways from this project.

- Vendor Support Matters: If you call vendor support for a business-critical issue and they cannot get you on the line with a technology expert within 30-minutes, you should look at moving to a vendor that does. There is nothing worse than non-responsive vendor support during a time of crisis.
- Cheap Solutions: The cheapest option is often not the best option. This is true for many things in life, if you want value, it will cost you.
- Crisis Management: Practice makes perfect. Test the plan and practice the process, including the roles within the recovery team. During a crisis there should be only one Crisis Manager calling the shots. Delegation is encouraged, but the team leaders should follow the direction of the Crisis Manager. It is easy to get tunnel vision and be sucked into the adrenalin of making decisions too quickly in a vortex of events. Every hour, the leadership team should take a few minutes to consider the big picture, decide if there is a better course of action, and make corrections if necessary. Only essential staff should be allowed in the crisis area.

Best Practices Are There for a Reason

"But this is how we have always done it!" I cannot tell you the number of times that I have heard that said by customers and partners....

One case involving a European service provider particularly stands out. The customer had already purchased the new system, and we were reviewing the service provider's proposal for the customer's ERP solution. Given that the list of approved and vetted systems for this ERP solution was relatively short, and the hardware was already purchased, there was not much that we could change.

Creating a proper solution for such environments is not trivial. You can bound your service offering to a point, but limit it too much and customers probably will not purchase your service. Make your offering too open, and you will have a difficult time standardizing and running things efficiently and effectively.

The Failure

We started by doing a review of what the service offering looked like. What were the requirements they designed the service against, what constraints were in place, and were the risks properly mitigated or at least documented? We discussed best practices written for the solution, and discussed availability and recoverability, as well as security. This conversation took place with several of the service provider's stakeholders.

But...have you ever noticed during a review that people from different teams make different assumptions about who does what, only to discover that these assumptions were not entirely correct.

> "Have you read our best practices guide?" asked one of my team members.
>
> "Why, yes, more than once" was the response from one of the customer stakeholders.

Unfortunately, reading a best practice guide does not help if you do not understand why the best practices are in place. Simply put, if you live in a country with right-hand traffic, you teach your kids to look "left-right-left" before they cross the streets. This makes sense, because the traffic they would first encounter comes from the left. If you understand why this best practice is in place you can adapt accordingly if you are in a country with left-hand traffic, and if you visit the United Kingdom, you look "right-left-right", avoid being run over by a London taxi.

The same logic applies to best practices in technology. Best practices are a good starting point and provide a setup that has been proven to work. But, depending on the environment, it might make sense to deviate from those settings. The tough part is gaining the insight that goes into a best practice guide, and filtering which settings are mandatory and which are optional.

The customer said, "We already have a VM with the application up and running that we can use to review." At first glance, the VM looked healthy. There was no load on the system, and it was just a test VM. Upon closer inspection, I noticed that something did not seem right. I typed `lsscsi` to look at the available SCSI devices, and it returned an error message: "Command not found." That was odd as all releases of the VM guest operating system that were verified by us, by default, contain the binary and properly run this command. A quick check for a release file in the `/etc` directory confirmed what I suspected. They had installed the VM with an operating system that the ERP provider did not support. When asked why they did this, the response came back promptly: "This is how we have always done it."

At that point, I decided to double-check various settings myself and verify that everything was implemented correctly. Unfortunately, "how we have always done it" turned out to be very much their practice. The computer system on which the VM ran used a Software Defined Storage (SDN) solution, where software handles policy-based provisioning and management of data storage independent of the hardware. The benefit of a centralized storage solution is that you can pack a vast number of physical disk drives together and present parts of their combined capacity to a server. That way, you may only see 1TB of disk capacity, but the usable space can be made up of hundreds of disks that can all service input and output requests in parallel. This is not the case with most software defined storage solutions.

This does not mean that you will not get excellent performance out of a software-defined storage solution, but in general, you need to work with multiple virtual disks to create parallel input and output streams. Unfortunately, because they were used to working with a minimal number of large disks, they only gave the system the bare minimum number of required disks.

NUMA (non-uniform memory access) can be simply described as a way to ensure that a computing process leverages the memory that is most local to the CPU where a process is running. This means that in a typical environment you configure a VM to stay within the physical boundaries. For example, if you have a physical CPU socket with 384 GB of memory attached to it and 20 cores, you should not create a VM with 512GB of memory or 30 cores. You must either stay within the physical boundaries of the physical socket or work with multiples to ensure maximum performance. The customer's VMs were all configured so that they either exceeded the number of locally available CPU cores or the locally available memory.

Unfortunately, this trend continued across almost all domains, including performance, recoverability, availability, management, security, and many more. Various departments had assumed the others would do the right thing, but ended up with an incorrect configuration. Also, everyone had read the best practices guide, but they failed to follow through on the recommendations, or they applied their own erroneous interpretations without fully understanding the background of the recommendations in the document.

How It Impacted My Customer

We were fortunate. We spotted a lot of the issues before the service provider went live with their first customer. With everything set up the way it was before my review, the result would have been catastrophic. Performance degradation would have been unavoidable. Even worse, the ERP provider would not have officially supported the entire environment because the customer used an unsupported OS. Nothing is worse than trying to get support when a system is misbehaving, only to then find out that the entire system is not supported!

What Could I Have Done Differently?

I made an assumption that people would comprehend what was written in the best practices guide and implement accordingly. Worst case, they would only knowingly implement deviations from the best practice recommendations for specific use cases. In this case, there was architecture in place for many years that worked relatively well. When the various components changed, without understanding new architecture, people reverted to what they already knew instead of following the best practices.

Also, I underestimated how strong the silos in the company were. Sometimes, all we have to do is pick up the phone to ask a simple question, but people in silos sometimes move forward without communicating with other groups even when they know they will get an unsatisfactory result.

What Did I Learn?

Sometimes you get lucky. In this case, the fact that we did not run into more serious issues after going live was pure good luck. If we had done the review a couple of weeks later this project would have taken a catastrophic turn. If possible, review your new environment before going live. This should be done in a project Discovery Phase, where the learning process leads to a systematic approach, including dealing with potential risks.

Talk to each other! Sometimes you must deal with the result of other people's work, and sometimes they do not want you to meddle in their processes. Even so, I recommend having a conversation about what you expect, or why and in what way you feel the delivered service is not fully useable. Sometimes the other department is not aware there is a mismatch, and if nothing else, it is a way to spend some time with and better understand the processes of a different department.

Additionally, when writing technical material for a different audience, have people from that audience proofread your material. In this case, we found items in our best practice guide that needed to be explained differently to different audiences, and a clear distinction was needed between which practices were mandatory versus items that could be changed by the customer.

Finally, there needs to be a balance between the information you need to give and how much you explain. The level of detail should be based on who is reviewing the material. The content areas may be different based on the different backgrounds of reviewers. This same consideration applies both for presenting and documenting material.

POC Stands for Production, Operation, and (scope) Creep

These were the early days of the VMware acquisition of DynamicOps company and their technology, DynamicOps Cloud Automation Center (DCAC) in 2012. The product was rebranded as VMware Cloud Automation Center (vCAC) before it was released to the customers. I was engaged as an architect to run a proof of concept (POC) in parallel with other consultants who were running different POCs in the same timeframe.

The Project

A partner company contacted ITAR sales to help with a long-term engagement for a Fortune 100 company (the customer) that involved a proper development of the automation and governance framework that specifies controls, standards, mechanisms, and any compliance requirements. However, the partner wanted to start the engagement with a POC for vCAC, vCloud Networking and Security (vCNS), and vCenter Operations Manager (vCOPS) for a Fortune 100 company, referred to as the customer in this story. Each of the POCs was to be completed in two weeks and they were all parallel streams to be completed simultaneously. One project manager was assigned to all three POCs. I was assigned as an architect to design and deploy the environment for vCAC. Another consultant was assigned to deploy vCNS, and a third consultant was to deploy vCOPS.

Also, the partner's sales team engaged ITAR sales to help their Business Services Unit (BSU) understand and define the customer's business goals, strategic goals, service definitions, cloud economics, flexibility, and intrinsic inter-operability.

The Failure

ITAR sales engaged the ITAR PSU Professional Services Unit (PSU) and BSU to help the partner on these various initiatives. Though it was treated as a single project, everything was identified as an individual initiative and a request was made for resource pooling.

ITAR PSU identified and assigned the architects, consultants and project managers for various IT initiatives, and ITAR BSU identified business consultants. No discussions were held regarding customer goals. Everything was done based on the SOWs that came in from the partner.

The customer's business and technical groups were engaged with various partner and ITAR teams based on their profile.

The Goals

All of these teams were in their own silos. Each team had clearly defined goals, but none of them were working together to define a common goal.

- The ITAR PSU goals were to complete POCs for the three streams.
- The ITAR BSU goals were to assist the partner's BSUs to understand the customer's business requirements.
- The goals of the partner and ITAR sales teams were to complete the project and seek opportunities to sell additional solutions and services to the customer.
- The customer business team wanted to properly define the services and provide a self-service cloud infrastructure for their business.
- The customer Information Technology team wanted to build a production-ready, self-service portal that they could use immediately to address their infrastructure needs.

Scope Creep: Phase 1

The purpose of my POC was to prove the concept that vCAC can automate the deployment of a VM or two with a self-service portal, as outlined in the SOW. During my initial discussions with the customer IT group, I quickly realized that they were looking for a production-ready environment so they could have a complete workload lifecycle.

I notified the ITAR sales team and project manager that the customer was asking for a production-ready environment with customization possibly required for the integration. This was not a POC and posed a risk of scope creep. I was told that time would not be a problem and I should do whatever was necessary.

I should have escalated further to make sure everyone understood the risks, but I thought it could be a good opportunity for both ITAR and me if all went well.

I started the knowledge transfer and data gathering sessions with the customer around vCAC architecture, including the requirements for the components (SQL Server, Manager Service Servers, Model Manager Servers (Web and Data), VMware Distributed Execution Manager (DEM) Orchestrators, DEM Workers, and vSphere Agents). After the design was determined and the customer provided the necessary Windows servers, including SQL servers, I installed and configured the software. There were a few environmental issues, but they seem to come with any Greenfield environment.

At this point, we were ready to build the first IaaS blueprint. Slowly, I realized that the customer had already used VM tags to customize many of their day-to-day operations such as custom VM names, backups, error notifications based on alarms and triggers, and so on. This was not going to be as simple as just building a blueprint from a basic template. They wanted to retain most of their custom functionality along with the new provisioning capabilities.

In parallel, the network team started working with the ITAR vCNS consultant and they realized that he did not have much vCNS API knowledge, so I got pulled into that stream as well to integrate vCNS into the vCAC blueprint definitions. In a way this was helpful as it gave me first-hand knowledge of what they were trying to do, but I had to shuffle my time between the two streams. The vCNS consultant left after two weeks, which was when the actual planning and implementation of the solution started.

And of course, it was not as simple as integrating some of the VLAN-backed L2 and L3 integration with some access control lists (ACLs). I worked with the customer's network team to come up with some creative ideas to standardize their virtual network provisioning.

The following types of vShield groups, and associated coverage areas, were identified:

- Global Systems Group – Enterprise servers.
- Application-specific Systems Groups – Systems groups with specific applications.
- Service Groups (Ports) – In and Out.

All of the newly provisioned systems would be added to Global Systems Group and checked against the VM Tags. Based on application property, a system would be added to those Application-specific Systems Groups. All of the systems (example: `All_Servers`) would be assigned to enterprise-grade common service groups (example: `ports-in` and `ports-out`), and some systems (example: `web_tier`) are assigned to additional service groups (example: `webtier_ports-in` and `webtier_ports-out`) based on specific applications.

After vShield groups had been identified, I created the necessary scripts calling out the vCNS API to be able to create a structure and then integrate it with vCAC using the Designer tool and vCO (vCenter Orchestrator) workflows. Of course, I realized that vCNS does not support appending to the firewall table, so I had to come up with new logic. Every time a new firewall rule was added it had to:

1. Add the new line to the script.
2. Clear the firewall rules.
3. Apply all the rules to the firewall.

This required a lot of time and effort.

After this was integrated with vCAC, I thought I was done. Based on customer requirements I had created a self-service portal with a service catalog that could provision VMs with necessary Network Layer 2 and 3 components, as well as all the ACLs.

Scope Creep: Phase 2

The customer's IT team said that the portal was not production-ready and was not what they wanted. They wanted it to be properly integrated with Active Directory, the IP Address Management (IPAM) solution, the load balancing solution, their ticketing system, the Configuration Management Database (CMDB), custom VM naming, and email notifications. And their list continued to grow....

At the same time, unknown to me, the sales team and ITAR's BSU were promising the customer's business teams that we could automate anything and everything they wanted. They did not realize that the original SOW was just a POC and had a limited scope.

Show Stopper

Concerned, I brought the new customer requirements to the attention of the ITAR sales team. They did not act surprised. They did not understand the scope and load impact, but despite this they said do whatever was necessary. I realized that I was doomed as a result of scope creep and this project had gone from a POC to a complete and customizable production deployment. Again, I should have escalated my concerns to a higher level, but my "can do" attitude led me to tackle the project anyway.

Though they seem simple now, I ran into several product and integration issues that had to be fixed at the engineering level through hot fixes. This was one of the first large-scale implementations after the product acquisition, so issues were expected. I worked on the following for the next few weeks:

- Custom VM name generation: Custom properties submitted during machine provisioning were utilized to build the logic for the VM name. The name was compared with Active Directory to verify it was not a duplicate. Then, the vCAC database was updated and the name was assigned to the new VM.
- Active Directory (AD) integration: This was not a straightforward request as there are several steps involving OU creation, distribution, and security groups. It also required adding VMs to the right OUs and to their required distribution groups based on VM properties defined during provisioning.
- IPAM integration: This initially seemed very straightforward. While provisioning a VM, I could call the API to get an IP address and register it with DNS. While deprovisioning a VM, I could unregister it from DNS and release the IP address used.
- Ticketing and CMDB systems: This involved several workflows, but I was able to integrate to the point where the basic functionality had been restored per customer requirements.
- Email notifications: These were initially used only for VM CPU and memory sizing notifications on a per organization and user basis.
- Load balancing integration: This was done so that whenever multiple IIS servers got deployed, they were backed by an application profile with a traffic type of HTTPS that supports the persistent types of cookie, SSL session ID (with SSL Passthrough enabled), and Source IP.

At this point, the blueprints were tested and I confirmed that all customer requests were completed. I had two working blueprints with all of the working customizations. Based on the customer's architectural and operational requirements the following had been configured: the tenants, fabric and resource reservation management, enterprise user grouping along with custom properties, property dictionaries, approval policies, and build/network/cost profiles.

I created all of the deliverables (though originally it was only a POC which does not normally include any deliverables). This was a complicated system and it was important that the customer had all of the necessary documentation for the design and customization logics so they could modify the design in the future if needed. Also, this documentation was shared with other ITAR consultants so they could make use of some of the standard customizations.

Scope Creep: Phase 3

Again, I thought I was done, but the customer's IT team again said that it was not production-ready and not completely what they were looking for. I was a little (just a little) surprised.

They said one of their requirements was to deploy a 57-machine system for one of their applications. They frequently deployed that application for a new location or a new development environment, and they needed a blueprint for it. They added that the customizations already in place were sufficient for the application and would not need any more.

I thought no big deal. I would create a new blueprint with those many machines pointing back to the necessary vSphere templates. There followed another few weeks of painful troubleshooting and resolution....

- Every time a 57-machine blueprint got provisioned, it waited for several minutes (sometimes hours) and then failed. Initially, I modified the blueprint with a smaller number of machines. For example, I started with 15, and then increased to 20, 25 and so on. The job was successful most of the time with a smaller number of machines, but the goal was 57.
- After reviewing several structured and unstructured data points of vCAC and other integration points, I realized that the deployed elements (DEM Workers) were waiting for a long time on the vCO workflows to complete. This was related to all of the external systems (AD, vCNS, IPAM, ticketing system, CMDB) timing out. By default, a DEM Worker can run up to 15 vCAC workflows in parallel, and queues up remaining workflows. I realized that the two DEM Workers were unable to scale for a job with several workflows tied to provisioning 57 machines. I requested and added four additional Windows servers and four additional DEM Workers. The jobs were then able to complete successfully.
- The following week when I went back to the customer site to wrap up the project, they mentioned that the new 57-machine blueprint was not consistent. It either completed or failed with a smaller number of machine deployments.
- For example, there will only be 17, 26, 34, or a random number of machines running and the rest of them fail.

After reviewing several logs (across the vCAC Manager Service, Web, and Agents), I found that the DEM workers were timing out waiting on their IPAM solution and the vCO workflows were failing to get an IP address for some machines.

I reviewed their IPAM solution and called the vendor only to discover that IPAM was failing because the IPAM API does not support more than one IP address/DNS registration per second. They were rewriting their API but the new version was months away and the current version could not be fixed. Because 57 machines were requesting IP addresses in just a few seconds, some of them were failing as the API could not handle so many at one time

To prevent more than one IP address or DNS registration occurring within the same second of time, I randomized the vCO workflow logic to stagger the deployments. I added a randomizer in my vCO workflow logic so there would not be more than one IP address or DNS registration request made within a second. This worked, and we were able to consistently provision several deployments.

I finally felt that I had fulfilled all of the customer requirements, including virtual network integration, several third-party integrations, and resolved product/solution issues. It felt really good that I had a satisfied customer at the end of a painful journey.

Scope Creep: Phase 4

Time to wrap up the project and move onto the next one, right? No, the customer had other plans! They said, “Hey, by the way, this was deployed on our Development subnet, can we move it to the production subnet?” And that is how I spent the rest of my life.... ☺

How It Impacted My Customer

Without proper planning ahead of the time between the customer’s business and technical teams, it was painful for the customer’s IT team as they were the end users utilizing the solution. The business team kept changing the course of actions based on their meetings, automation assumptions, discussions, and experiences without consulting with the technical teams. This led to a lot of frustration for the customer’s technical teams.

Though, I helped with the majority of the technical work, the customer’s technical teams still had to determine how to deal with the ever-changing requirements based on what they needed versus what the business owners wanted. The customer should have stepped back and formed a Center of Excellence with all of their business and technical teams. They should have figured out the requirements of the project and how to handle the deployment and operational aspects going forward with the introduction of automation and orchestration.

What Could I Have Done Differently?

I experienced a lot of pain during the course of the project as things kept changing or piling up on one another, but I was ultimately satisfied with the results. This does not mean I could not have done things differently to improve the process. I could have done the following better:

- Escalation and Push back: This project had serious scope creep (I saw them as a flood of new/random requests). I recognized this early and tried to push back, unsuccessfully, at every step or phase of the project. I could have escalated to the highest level to halt the project so that it would be properly scoped from the beginning. However, I later learned that because the customer's business and technical teams were not in sync, that would not have helped in defining determining a properly defined scope. At least, it would have provided more time to determine what the customer was trying to achieve.

  I still say the mantra "POC is never for Production" 10 times a day.

- Phased Approach: I should have paused, realized there were various workstreams being simultaneously executed for the same project, and generated a showstopper. The business requirements should all have been defined prior to the technical design and implementation, not simultaneously. This would have solved the issues, as we would have had clear business requirement details supporting the design and implementation of the solution. However, the customer had to wait for a few months to get their environment up and running.

- Run away: I could have run away when I initially disagreed with the scope of the project and how it was potentially disastrous, but was that really an option? I ended up taking on the challenge and learned from it.

What Did I Learn?

On the one hand, I learned that I should not move forward with a POC if I sense scope creep, and should immediately escalate to the highest level necessary before proceeding.

On the other hand, if I had escalated and halted the project, none of the great work that went into this project would have been done by me. The bug fixes that went into the products would have taken a long time, and all the integrations and knowledge transfer might not have been shared with ITAR's Professional Services unit. The VMworld presentation about this project (a case study of architectural reviews, implementation and integrations, and how it helped lead other engagements) would not have happened.

I see positivity in everything. The project was very painful at points, but I still succeeded and ended up with a happy customer. When things are out of your control, just put in your 110% and you will be fine.

Smell the Roses

One of the most rewarding things I have done is to rise to the level in my career where I am looked to for guidance by my peers. I find that helping others gives me that protagonist feeling that motivates me to do even more on a day-to-day basis. The positive feeling and confidence that comes when you are working hard to reach a goal and everything starts to fall into place is unsurpassed. And it is addictive. You find yourself always chasing that next project and striving to make it better than the last one, but this can consume you and makes you vulnerable.

The Dilemma

A dilemma was presented to me by a colleague about one of her customers, ITAR, and how their technical support staff repeatedly broke their PCs when making software changes. I thought this seems like a pretty small issue…just tell them to stop doing what they are doing. If only it were that simple. After you know the full context of the issues, you understand that there is a "people coefficient," and just telling someone to stop doing something does not mean they will. Planning for the people coefficient is often overlooked, but it is an essential part of any solution. And if your personality is like mine it can also send you into a spiraling attempt to make something perfect.

I continually thought about this discussion. My brain was consumed with trying to solve this problem during meetings, while talking to friends, at the dinner table, and while lying in bed at night staring at the ceiling. It was not even my problem! I knew that this could be solved with an IT solution or better management, but what was the right approach? Why was I consumed with this?

This situation was not new for me. It happens all the time. I get hyper-focused on a path to resolution. I think of ways to fix the problem, and also ways to ignore it. It is a constant internal struggle. I keep a notebook by my bedside table drawer so I can get thoughts out of my head and onto paper at night, and hopefully get some sleep too.

The following morning, I was irritable and cranky because of the lack of sleep, and I took it out on my family. My conversations were short, making coffee took too long, and even my playful dog did not get me out of this mood. I just wanted to get on with my day—why can people not understand this? The ride to work that day was just like any other day, self-consumed. Thankfully, the car knew how to get me to work, because the ride was a blur.

I approached my colleague when I got to work and asked for more background information about the issue. The first thing she said was "do not worry about it." If she only knew how the last 24 hours had been for me! I pushed back, wanting to know the whole situation, and injected myself into her problem because I had spent all of the previous day and night wondering how to get those employees to a workable solution.

She told me about the customer service group and how they supported a suite of software products when ITAR's customers called in for help. ITAR's customers might have any version of the software, and it was rare that any two customers had similar setups. In this support model, the customers' computers were not always managed by ITAR, and there could be anything from Candy Crush to their kids' homework, or malware, on these PCs.

Every call was different. When customers called in to support, they explained their problem to the customer service technician, and most cases were solved quickly. But, when the user had a more difficult problem, or needed assistance with an upgrade or to move the software to a new PC, issues occurred. Though I am not a customer service person, I worked on a help desk for various companies and can relate to both the customer and the technician. We have all called in for assistance at some point, and have had both great and some not so great experiences.

ITAR support technicians strive to provide the best possible customer experience, and as part of that effort had been corrupting their productivity tool, their PC. My colleague explained how the customer service technicians continually installed and uninstalled software on their PC in an effort to replicate the customer's issue, trying to give themselves as much knowledge and understanding of a problem as possible. This was awesome as they were really going out of their way to provide the best possible experience—I loved this company! They were helping customers the way they themselves would want to be helped. You cannot fault them for that.

However, this practice of continually installing and uninstalling software had adverse effects. Services such as email and instant messaging encountered problems, ITAR support technicians needed more time to work their issues, and it had become a nightmare for the single IT support staff member at one location. Given employee time lost when their PC was down, and increasing call wait times for the customers, the practice was not sustainable.

I live for challenges, and this was a good one. My colleague asked "So what do you think we can do?" This was a trigger sentence, just like when you ask your dog, "Do you want to go out?" after you have just arrived home after a 10-hour day. I told her I would get back to her with some thoughts. My day was already full at this point, and the rest of the week looked the same, and it was only Tuesday...

Meeting after meeting went by, and all the while thoughts about how to solve this problem were still foremost in my mind. 5:30 p.m.... I forced myself to head home, frustrated that I could not finish that one last thing. I got home, said hi to the wife and kids, grabbed a snack, and went to my home office to finish what I had left behind. I thought to myself fifteen minutes is all I need to finish this while it is fresh in my head. After 35 minutes, dinner was over, the kids were hanging out, and I was still in my office. I went downstairs and played a game with the kids, but I was not fully present. I watched the TV with the family, but I did not hear it. I was still consumed and could not stop thinking about the problem.

The kids went to bed, and I went back to my home office to work on the issue. It was late and I had already been at it for 11 hours, so I just planned to take a few minutes and get some ideas into my notebook. Another two hours went by. My wife was in bed, I was hungry and tired, I had not fully solved the problem, and I felt defeated.

I initially tried to solve the problem from a heavy-handed IT point of view by trying to figure out how to lock the PC down so that the user could not make changes to it. I tested hundreds of group policies to turn things off. I researched, downloaded, installed, and reviewed different types of software that claimed to revert users' changes. Blogs were read, Google was searched, and I listened to podcasts in the car to find the best approach and practice to keep these employees from doing anything I did not like or that IT did not like.

It was a perfect picture of stupid when I was done! Software had to be white-listed to be installed or run. Users were in a monochrome world, a dystopian computing environment where IT said what you could do and how you should do it. It was embarrassing to think that I could build such a monster when we are trying to foster an IT landscape where users have choice. Thankfully, I came to my senses and realized that I should approach this from ITAR’s perspective. Their support technicians were providing exceptional customer service. The only problem was their PC.

I thought about running a local hypervisor with a virtual machine that they could revert to a snapshot whenever they wanted to start over. But, this brought up additional questions such as whether the support technicians were technical enough to work with this new software, were their PCs fast enough to run it, and would they be concerned that this would increase their support calls. This approach would work technically, but it would not work for the users. There was a better way.

The Project

Virtual desktops hosted in the datacenter, with an easy-to-use interface for end users, would solve most of the issues. The plan was developed and presented to my colleague who championed it with her customer. A pilot was agreed upon, and we built out the first iteration. Over the following weeks we developed the platform, made changes to how things performed within the operating system, and prepared instructions for end users so that we would be ready to go live.

During the pilot we got feedback that it worked really well, but there were questions about making the necessary, already installed in-house software more responsive. We made some adjustments, and even built additional virtual machines that housed multiple versions of the software to decrease the amount of time ITAR's support technicians had to spend preparing to support each customer. The technicians could continue using their PCs in their usual way and when launching a virtual desktop, there was zero impact to the PC.

The Failure

We provided each user with a dedicated VM for their work, but they needed assistance reverting the machines when they became unusable. This required opening an IT ticket with the help desk, which was then reviewed and escalated to the appropriate team to revert the snapshot. This was initially OK, but as adoption grew, the need to revert the machines became more frequent and the time from the request to delivery became progressively longer.

Later, I finally had a great solution to the problem: non-persistent virtual desktops. A decision was made to move from dedicated virtual machines to non-persistent desktops that vaporized on logout and were replaced with fresh systems ready for consumption. We had previously worked with a staff member to build out the dedicated desktops, so the templates were ready to go. We built the non-persistent virtual desktops and provided a floating pool for the agents to pull from, again using the same front end from the dedicated desktop version. The user experience was immediately better. The users did not require IT to reset the systems; they only needed to logout. They could use multiple versions of the software on multiple virtual machines, and when their shift was done and they logged out, new systems were automatically built. The automation component did its job, and as an additional benefit, the security footprint was smaller because they were now non-persistent virtual desktops.

How It Impacted My Customer

Starting off with a pilot where each of the support staff had a dedicated desktop was a mistake. If we had started with non-persistent desktops, we could have saved a month or two of work, and gotten through this project much quicker.

What Could I Have Done Differently?

This project had its pain points and to say we just got it done would not be true. It is not easy to work through the challenges from a first line worker's point of view when you are embedded in the IT consulting space with an administrator's perspective. You must be able to change your perspective.

If I had first walked through the end-user's day-to-day routine with them, perhaps I would have seen the workflow requirements earlier and started out with non-persistent desktops. If I had seen how often they need to reset their desktops, and how long it took (using the existing processes) to reset a desktop, it would have been obvious that non-persistent desktops would be the right answer for their workflow.

What Did I Learn?

I learned that it is important to talk with all of the stakeholders and users, including in this case the customer support staff. It was great that the stakeholders had buy in, but until I saw how the solution was consumed by the customer support staff, I did not realize my initial solution of persistent desktops would not fully fix the problem. Always carve out some time to work with the people who will actually use the solution you are designing!

The other thing I learned was the importance of time management and making sure you know your priorities, including personal priorities. I did improve the call interaction times, but did I remember to eat lunch? I found a creative way to keep the help desk staff reimage laptops for the customer support team, but did I remember my wife's birthday or our anniversary? I had time commitments in this project, but what about that accumulated vacation time that never gets used? You can work long into the night after a full day of work, and sacrifice your personal time to get something right, but what about that promise to play a game with the kids tonight?

Maintaining a work-life balance is something we all cheer when we hear our employer talk about it, but it is up to us to see that it gets done…and few of us do.

Finding that work/life balance is something that most of us overlook. During this project, it became front and center for me. Remember…it is OK to have passion for your work. Most of us in IT enjoy our jobs. Just do not lose sight of what is important. Take time to smell the roses!

> "Don't spend so much time making a living
> that you forget to have a life."

- Unknown

The Digital Transformation Journey to the Cloud

> "Change is the law of life, and those who look only to the past or present are certain to miss the future." —John F. Kennedy

Change is a constant, a natural part of any journey. ITAR's CEO had decided that their digital transformation journey would be a multi-year effort to be completed in two Phases. Phase I was about digital transformation for outsourcing IT, and Phase II was about going to the cloud.

The plan and strategy for the first phase was to outsource the IT department. On paper, this appeared to be a good idea. Why not? If both partnering companies and competitors were cutting costs and doing more with less to be competitive, it seemed like a good direction. Employees are a company's most significant expense and outsourcing could reduce the cost. In hindsight, outsourcing is not a panacea and things could have gone a lot better....

The Failure

The Phase I outsourcing of the majority of the ITAR IT department was completed in about 18 months. The Phase II contracts had already been signed, but the outsourcing company failed to provide a functional architecture and design, and the project timeline was already slipping. There were no fully developed or documented standards or guidelines. The outsourcing company did not have the knowledge and experience necessary to deliver the solution.

A geek at heart, a technologist and principal consultant by trade; I was the lead consultant, a cloud architect, tasked with creating and developing the Cloud Center of Excellence. My primary responsibility was to help architect, design, and create standards and guidelines for the cloud infrastructure foundation.

Instantly, I also became the de-facto program manager and project manager. Fortunately for me, the sole managing cloud director (my primary customer stakeholder) was a gifted former developer who understood infrastructure. He had recruited an Intel and Windows server whiz kid with a developer background who had a great passion for DevOps. The “Three Amigos” picked up the pieces and architected, designed, and documented everything for the Cloud Foundation Work, including driving and guiding the outsourcing company to deliver the architecture and design we created.

The outsourcing company was a traditional GUI–focused workforce with conventional datacenter operational experience. They had no cloud experience. This was one of the biggest challenges, and because of it an additional 12-months of effort was required to get from proof of concept to being live and fully operational. Our work was vital in getting Phase II delivered before the end of the year.

How It Impacted My Customer

Some Enterprises still have in-house IT functions with siloed business units. This is not good. Many large enterprises have already outsourced most of their IT functions, including architecture, engineering, and operations. In many cases, outsourcing just made things worse.

In our case, outsourcing resulted in a bad experience. We paid the outsourcing company that was managing our on-premises environment to develop our Cloud Foundations, and it was like pulling teeth without anesthesia. They did not understand the cloud and did not have the expertise needed to deliver the solution. We ended up defining the Cloud Foundations ourselves, and had to be very specific about how to do the deployment and build-out.

Many enterprises have run into this same outsourcing issue. The recommendation is that if you decide to outsource, outsource the operations, and keep internal architecture and engineering teams. Or, get rid of the underperforming outsourcer all together and bring in a specialty outsourcer that knows cloud and can deliver. Neither option was available to us, so we had to mentor and educate the original outsourcer.

What Could I Have Done Differently?

Based on my experience and the lessons I learned from this project I would do the following things differently:

- Before you venture into the cloud, understand the outsourcing providers skill set, certifications, and accreditations with cloud.
- Get references and speak to outsourcer customers they are currently serving. Look for customers who have a similar environment to yours or have achieved the desired state.
- Consider bringing architecture and engineering teams back in-house.
- Understand your workload profiles and the applications.
- Understand networking requirements and plan for growth.
- Try to run SaaS and PaaS services to leverage the cloud provider as much as possible.
- Run IaaS only when required (when SaaS/PaaS cannot solve your business requirement).
- Training.

What Did I Learn?

I experienced many challenges and issues on this project. The following are some considerations that may help to avoid difficult situations and pitfalls, and some tips to help remediate issues.

Do Not Make Temporary Fixes

Avoid ad-hoc, point-in-time fixes as they are fragile and cause issues later. Temporary fixes are workarounds and are not intended to be permanent. Workarounds can take on a life of their own and become permanent due to various factors, including:

- Lack of funding and budget cuts.
- Lack of documentation.
- People deploy things into production and then leave the company.

The key is to automate everything you can and deploy IaC (Infrastructure as Code). The benefits are high as you can do versioning, and the YAML and JSON files provide real live up-to-date documentation. Also, you can control and reiterate and know what you changed, and others can see what you did and how you did it.

The Blame Game Poisons the well

The blame game and pointing fingers at others does not solve anything—it makes things worse. Having a DevOps culture and performing blameless post-incident reviews allows for finding and remediating issues so they do not become recurring issues. Develop a culture of trust and a reward process to encourage people to find bugs.

Dream Big!

The DevOps, Agile, CI/CD pipeline requires dreaming big because it requires a culture change for most enterprises. If you dream small and get only 30%-50% done you have made progress, but not enough. Dreaming big gets you a lot further down the road.

Culture Change Is Hard

We know culture change is hard. Performing business as usual does not help with change and is counterproductive to DevOps and cloud initiatives.

If It Does Not Work On-Premises Do Not Put It in the Cloud

Governance and optimized workloads require thoughtful effort and multiple reiterations to continuously improve. Chances are it will cost you more if you are "lifting and shifting" a bad application with an inadequate process to the cloud. Just shifting it to the cloud does not improve the application or the process.

Summary

Understand your business requirements and reasons for moving to the cloud. The cloud is not a panacea. Due diligence is required, and you need to understand how to leverage cloud-native workloads and if and when to migrate workloads to the cloud. Again, this is a hybrid multi-cloud world and not all workloads belong in the cloud. In this journey, everyone's experience will be different. Hopefully, some of the lessons related in this story can help with your cloud journey.

Building Bridges to Success

This story is focused on the lessons learned in moving through the roles and ranks in the infrastructure design and administration space. As such, there is not one specific failure or use case. It provides insights that complement other stories in this book and includes lessons learned as I advanced through several certifications on my journey to becoming an IT architect. It also provides insight into why approach matters.

Some of the reasons I originally wanted to become an architect were less than noble. I thought...I will not have to explain my decisions to others, I will not be questioned, and I will not be as ignorant as they are. There are contradictions within these thoughts and I hope your motivations for wanting to progress are more noble than mine were at that time, be they career development, recognition and visibility, or whatever positively motivates you.

The Failure

What triggered my journey was my role as second-line support for VMware environments. With less than a year experience, occupied with support calls, internal tickets, and a lot of overtime, I realized that it was a road to nowhere. I was digging deeper and deeper, and felt like I was losing sight of the bigger picture. I did not have the knowledge and skill sets that I needed to work at a more advanced level.

The Value of Continuous Development

A new team member who was very focused on certification joined our team. He encouraged me to aspire and recommended that I find time for self-development. I took his advice and prepared for the VMware Certified Advanced Professional Administration exam. It took months of exhausting work to pass the exam, but it increased my capabilities and confidence. Then, I started to think about passing the Design exam. By the time I started preparing for it, I saw that there was a lot more to design than just log analysis, support cases, and typical day-to-day operational activities.

Design Exams

The VMware Design exams are totally different from Deploy exams. Design exams focus on architecture rather than operational aspects, and take a holistic approach towards business requirements. Believe me, for a guy that was all about deploying new VMware ESXi servers (doing patching, log analysis, updates, and so on), this was a great transition.

The learning process for any design exam provides tremendous value. You learn how to engage with business stakeholders as a design professional to help them move forward with their business initiatives. As a certified design professional, I would help stakeholders meet their business goals.

In my opinion, VMware Design Exams (and VCDX) use the best available IT architecture frameworks that apply to existing and emerging VMware technologies and are well-suited for Solution or Domain IT Architects. Questions about manageability, availability, lifecycle, recoverability, and security are addressed. This applies to VMware vSphere environments, private clouds, public clouds, and hybrid clouds. There are different tools to achieve the goals, but the framework is so flexible it can be used across many practice areas. As you work towards an architect position, be aware that technologies will change during your career and you need to stay up to date. As you acquire new certifications and competencies you become a more valuable resource, and it becomes more likely that you will be the first to be deployed to deal with new technologies, conduct proofs of concept, and implement business initiatives.

Approach Matters

I remember my first project as a member of technical staff. The project was not even close to completion as the deadline neared, and each day brought more issues. Some issues were escalated to the management team as the project became endangered and failed to meet the project timeline.

I was the newcomer and least experienced team member on the project, but was not fully utilized and had some available time. I started to act as a spokesperson for virtualization, storage, backup solutions, and other technologies used by a department in the company. The project manager and lead architect appreciated having a single point of contact to directly channel or outsource some of the work. The other technical people were happy because they wasted less time in pointless meetings. I took responsibility for more than was required, and it was a win-win for both parties.

Even better, when the next project came up with the same project manager and architects, they asked my manager to assign me to their project. They asked me for help in my areas of expertise, and started passing positive comments about me to other departments. As a result, I became involved in even more projects. I had only an engineering title, but I played at a table of equals. I listened, contributed, and helped where needed. An engineering title is valuable, but communication skills become increasingly important as you take on more responsibility in your career.

While attending VMworld Europe in 2018, I went to a session about Career Development called "Achieving Happiness: Building Your Brand and Your Career" (LDT1907BE) presented by Amanda Blevins and Joe Baguley. To paraphrase something Amanda said, "The Room will speak about you, when you leave it." Leaving people with a positive experience and impression is something I strive for and is part of being a successful IT architect.

A Sense of Accomplishment

I felt a sense of accomplishment. I had helped to create something new, with real value. I had graduated beyond moving tickets to creating new solutions. My background and commitment to learning helped me better understand the issues and the approaches to resolve them.

Eric Shanks wrote a blog post about sense of accomplishment within IT titled “Are You Proud of What You have Done?”(https://theithollow.com/2017/01/30/proud-youve-done/) If you are thinking about becoming an architect, you might find yourself involved with activities similar to those Eric describes. I encourage you to read his blog post as it also discusses IT career development during times with ground-breaking technologies on the horizon.

Communication Skills

I obtained a new skill-set of external (business) communication from the design workshops. I was able to use my new communication skills even within my own team to ask important questions and challenge the current state.

I remember a discussion with a storage administrator about a new storage array and a new software version. Old arrays could not update to the new version due to “lifecycle stuff.” He noted that the new software would provide a new GUI and CLI features. I asked the administrator, “Please explain why our company should spend millions of dollars just to improve the user experience.” The answer was silence.

It was not my intent to put down the storage administrator’s idea. He had a good reason why he wanted a new solution, but he did not articulate it in a manner that was compelling to our CFO and business stakeholders. I suggested that he build a business story behind this purchase and explain why it is needed, how it would improve company life, and how it would improve the experience for customers hosted on legacy solutions. With such story-telling, chances are much better that the customer would acquire these new features.

Social Networking

While you are gaining recognition within an organization you may discover that there are more people like you. (“Great minds think alike.”) There are other colleagues who will cross boundaries to do more than their position requires. These like-minded people are resources with whom you can consult, validate ideas, discuss technical decisions, and cross-check or verify your opinions. And even if they cannot directly help, they may refer you to someone that can. Social networking is a crucial activity that enables you to build a network of contacts that can help each other when needed. This is not limited to only technical subject matter experts, but also includes project managers, stakeholders, and friends!

What Did I Learn?

I have come to realize that being an IT architect is not a role—it is a mindset.

If you are on the journey to become an IT architect consider the following:

- Continue your technical development. Aim for advanced certification. You will learn a lot during the process, and apply your new knowledge sooner than you think.
- Do more than is expected from you in your current role. Look for areas where you can contribute, and work to earn positive recognition within your organization.
- Network with colleagues. Build friend and peer networks inside and outside of your organization. Make yourself available to peers and teams so they know they can depend on your help.
- Develop soft (people and communication) skills. These are the most underestimated skill sets of all!

All of these tools, skills, approaches, and assets can be used at any position, and within any organization.

Stories from the Field: Retrospective

Let us conclude with a retrospective.

There are many stories, and many potential conclusions that can be drawn for each. I have read from the start of each story through to the final edits that included input from other contributors, and some ghost writing by Matthew and me.

The original working title of the book was "Horror stories from the field," because we initially focused on the major disasters in running a project.

As more stories came in, many included more than one specific failure in a project. They uncovered interesting dynamics, and a thread emerged that multiple things lead to major failures. This is similar to what I read in a book by Sidney Dekkar, titled "Drift into Failure: From Hunting Broken Components to Understanding Complex Systems."[5] Compound errors led to many of the failures faced by the contributors in their work. In each case, a retrospective reviews the areas that could have been improved, and the lessons learned.

We hope you learned from these stories, and had fun reading them.

For those interested in participating in volume 2 of this *Stories from the Field* mini-series, please contact the IT Architect Resource team at itaseries.com. This book provides a model for story types and structures. Contributors will be given instructions and a template to use when writing your story.

Thank you again for the contributions and team work leading up to this release, and best wishes for success and future collaboration!

John Yani Arrasjid

---

[5] Drift Into Failure: From Hunting Broken Components to Understanding Complex Systems, 1st Edition, Sidney Dekkar, CRC Press, 2011, ISBN 978-1409422211

IT Architect Series and Other Works

The following are publications in the IT Architect Series and other works by the editors and colleagues.

IT Architect Series

The IT Architect Series of books is published by IT Architect Resource, LLC. Our mission is to publish books that benefit the reader as a resource, a reference, a teaching tool, and as entertainment in relation to the IT Infrastructure Design field.

- *Foundation in the Art of Infrastructure Design*, Arrasjid, Gabryjelski, Chris McCain, 2016. A practical guide for IT architects. ISBN: 978-0-9966477-4-8 (sc), 978-0-9966477-1-7 (hc), 978-0-9966477-3-1 (eBook).
- *Designing Risk in IT Infrastructure*, Daemon Behr, 2017. Understand the relationships between risk response, resources, cost and acceptance.
- *The Journey*, Melissa Palmer, 2018. A guidebook for anyone interested in IT architecture. ISBN: 978-0-9990929-0-3.
- *Stories from the Field, Vol. 1*, Contributors listed at itaseries.com and editors Wood/Arrasjid/Gabryjelski, 2020. A collection of short stories of projects gone wrong with lessons learned. (This book.)

Other Works

- *VMware vCloud Architecture Toolkit*, VMware Press, 2014. The complete vCAT printed reference: knowledge, tools, and validated designs for building high-value vCloud solutions. Includes contributors to this book (John Yani Arrasjid, Raman Veeramraju, Matthew Wood)
- *VCDX Boot Camp, Preparing for the VCDX Panel Defense*, VMware Press, 2013. Arrasjid, Lin, Khalil.

- *Cloud Computing with VMware vCloud Director*, USENIX Association Short Topics in System Administration #24, Arrasjid, Lin, Veeramraju, Kaplan, Epping, Haines, 2011. ISBN-13: 978-1-931971-83-6.
- *Foundation for Cloud Computing with VMware vSphere 4*, USENIX Association Short Topics in System Administration #21, Arrasjid, Epping, Kaplan, 2011. ISBN-13: 978-1-931971-83-6.
- *Deploying the VMware Infrastructure*, USENIX Association Short Topics in System Administration #18, Arrasjid, Balachandran, Conde, Lamb, Kaplan, 2008. ISBN-13: 978-1-931971-62-1.
- *The Buffalo Font Catalogue, Version 4*, George L. Sicherman, Revised by John Y. Arrasjid, 1986. Technical report 86-13.

Reader Services

Visit the book website:

http://itaseries.com

or

http://www.itarchitectseries.com

Register this book for convenient access to any updates, downloads, or errata that might become available.

About the Editors and the Artist

Matthew Wood is an independent technical writer with a 47-year career that has spanned telecommunications, UNIX, Linux, virtualization, cloud, professional services, and IT management applications. He has worked in many roles from computer operator to datacenter manager, usability engineer, and technical writer and editor.

Matthew was the lead technical writer and later managed the VMware Technical Services publications group, and was editor-in-chief for the vCAT project from 2010 until 2013. He wrote the original documentation to support tools such as VMware HealthAnalyzer and Migration Manager. Matthew also assisted John Arrasjid and others as an editor on the USENIX books *Deploying the VMware Infrastructure* and *Cloud Computing with VMware vCloud Director.*

John Yani Arrasjid is currently CTO at Ottometric, Inc., a startup focused on intelligent validation of systems and sensors in the automotive space using AI, Computer Vision, and Deep Learning to increase accuracy, shorten analysis time, and reduce cost. He has spent a lifetime working as an innovation architect and technical evangelist in the roles of senior technologist, principal architect, CTO, and CIO.

John is co-founder of the *IT Architect Series*. John is an author with multiple publishing houses on multiple technical topics. He has worked on patents covering workload modeling, blockchain, and accelerator resource management. John served as USENIX Association Board of Directors VP from 2010-2016. He has participated in Community Emergency Response Team (CERT) efforts since 2016, having FEMA certifications, corporate Medical Emergency Response Teams (MERT), and Burning Man Dispatch operations experience.

John continues his interest in IT architecture, and areas related to autonomous systems and sensors with AI, IoT, and Big Data. Twitter: @vcdx001

Ioannis Dangerous Age, is the legendary record cover artist and art designer for legendary bands such as Deep Purple, Allman Brothers Band, Styx, Lynyrd Skynyrd, Uriah Heep, King Crimson, Yngwie Malmsteen, Dokken, Blue Oyster Cult, Fates Warning, Mountain, Saga, Dream Theater, Sepultura, Biohazzard, Johnny Winter, The Tubes, UFO, and many more. In 2010 he designed a limited edition print for Furthur's (Bob Weir, Phil Lesh) appearance at Radio City Music Hall New York that was signed by Ioannis and Bob Weir. Recently. he also started a 20 plus volume set for legendary classic rock band Uriah Heep and created a series of paintings that grace the best-selling book *Get The Led Out: How Led Zeppelin Became the Biggest Band in the World*, published in 2012. He also is the co-author of *Fade To Black* with Martin Popoff a collection of the best hard rock cover artwork of the vinyl era also published in 2012.

To obtain a signed fine art print of the cover artwork, please go to www.dangerousage.com/store/ where you will be able to select this and other collectable merchandise designed by the artist IOANNIS.

Mark Gabryjelski (VCDX-023) has focused on solutions design and integration for clients since 1996. With a datacenter optimization focus, he has worked across all customer business aspects. Mark's leadership at Worldcom Exchange, extends to mentoring and sharing his technical capabilities with Professional Services and leadership teams. He combines his IT architecture skills and projects leadership from concept to completion. Including forklift upgrades with minimal impact. Mark has been involved in New England area user groups since 2006. He encourages others to think outside the box, to better themselves and their team, and to share their collaborative results.

Mark holds IT certifications from Cisco, Dell/EMC, HP, IBM, Microsoft, Nutanix, Veeam, and VMware. He is a VMware SME in Datacenter Virtualization, Desktop & Mobility, and Digital Business Transformation. Mark is VCP #46 and VCDX #23. The VCDX (VMware Certified Design Expert) certification requires a review by your peers prior to being awarded this title.

Mark is an author of *Foundation in the Art of IT Infrastructure Design* and co-founder of the *IT Architect Series*.
Twitter: @MarkGabbs.